Mediating Imperfect AI

AF764110

Carolina Escudero

Mediating Imperfect AI

Journalists' Emotional Responses to Technological Disruption

palgrave
macmillan

Carolina Escudero
Journalism School
University of Missouri
Barcelona, Catalonia, Spain

ISBN 978-3-032-01289-0 ISBN 978-3-032-01290-6 (eBook)
https://doi.org/10.1007/978-3-032-01290-6

© The Editor(s) (if applicable) and The Author(s), under exclusive license to Springer Nature Switzerland AG 2025

This work is subject to copyright. All rights are solely and exclusively licensed by the Publisher, whether the whole or part of the material is concerned, specifically the rights of translation, reprinting, reuse of illustrations, recitation, broadcasting, reproduction on microfilms or in any other physical way, and transmission or information storage and retrieval, electronic adaptation, computer software, or by similar or dissimilar methodology now known or hereafter developed.
The use of general descriptive names, registered names, trademarks, service marks, etc. in this publication does not imply, even in the absence of a specific statement, that such names are exempt from the relevant protective laws and regulations and therefore free for general use.
The publisher, the authors and the editors are safe to assume that the advice and information in this book are believed to be true and accurate at the date of publication. Neither the publisher nor the authors or the editors give a warranty, expressed or implied, with respect to the material contained herein or for any errors or omissions that may have been made. The publisher remains neutral with regard to jurisdictional claims in published maps and institutional affiliations.

Cover illustration: Mirtha Bermegui

This Palgrave Macmillan imprint is published by the registered company Springer Nature Switzerland AG
The registered company address is: Gewerbestrasse 11, 6330 Cham, Switzerland

If disposing of this product, please recycle the paper.

To Thomas, for your unwavering support.
To Danton, for the light you always bring.

Preface

Professional experience in journalism has consistently informed and shaped my academic inquiry into media, journalism, and media psychology. Over the years, these reflections have increasingly focused on the emotional and ethical dimensions of journalistic practice, particularly within an era defined by rapid technological change and the expanding presence of artificial intelligence (AI) across media ecosystems. This book emerges at the intersection of these concerns and is guided by a central question: How do journalists feel in the present moment, amid the disruptive arrival of AI?

Asking how journalists feel in the present moment connects directly to the notion of *ser-estando*, a concept drawn from the philosophical work of Rodolfo Kusch (1976). This term describes an ontological and existential mode of being that is inseparable from one's social, cultural, and historical contexts. When placed in dialogue with Arlie Hochschild's (1983) sociology of emotional labor, this conceptual framework enables a deeper reflection on the emotional dimensions of journalistic practice—specifically, the emotions that are expected, regulated, or suppressed in the newsroom (Huxford & Hopper, 2020; Kotišová, 2020; Ivask et al., 2023). It also reaffirms the enduring significance of critical thought, ethical responsibility, and emotional awareness in a profession increasingly shaped by algorithms, automation, and accelerated technological processes.

My first formal steps in journalism took place at TEA (Taller, Escuela, Agencia) in Argentina, pursued alongside initial studies in sociology at the University of Buenos Aires. Although those studies in sociology remained unfinished due to my relocation to France, they helped cultivate an early interest in the intersections between media practice and social inquiry. My training later continued at the *grande école de journalisme* CUEJ (Centre Universitaire d'Enseignement du Journalisme) in Strasbourg, where I completed my degree in journalism. During my final year, I participated in a capstone research project that took me to Belgrade, Serbia, alongside a cohort of classmates to report on post-conflict society.

In the town of Pančevo, amid depopulated neighborhoods and the remnants of bombed-out buildings, I encountered for the first time the profound complexities of reporting from a post-war landscape. As Şahin (2021) argues, such environments confront journalists with intricate professional identities, contested role perceptions, and significant ethical challenges particularly in contexts where peace remains fragile and social divisions endure. During my time there, I interviewed survivors of armed conflict, whose testimonies were shaped by long silences, distant gazes, and the painstaking labor of memory. Some shared their experiences with striking clarity; others struggled to find the words to articulate their pain and perspectives. These encounters left a lasting impression on me. Empathy and a deep sense of responsibility (Stupart, 2021) were not only clearly present, but became intertwined with a range of other emotions that I began to recognize within myself especially while transcribing the interviews (Lecheler, 2020; Pantti & Wahl-Jorgensen, 2021).

In those moments—and long afterward—I asked myself: Who was I to request that others relive their trauma through my questions? To speak of what they had lost and could never recover? I had not survived war—they had—and that realization fundamentally shifted my understanding of the journalistic profession. The discomfort I felt during those interviews became the foundation for a deeper awareness: that journalistic ethics and objectivity, while essential, are not sufficient. I came to recognize that greater knowledge in psychology, gender studies, and social psychology could be helpful and offer meaningful support in such encounters. What emerged was a conviction that further education was necessary, not only to refine my technical skills, but also to cultivate a more profound, empathetic understanding of the Other: their needs, their silences, and their dignity.

This formative experience set the course for the academic and professional journey that followed. I later worked in a range of media organizations and educational institutions across North America, Latin America, and Europe, actively seeking opportunities to challenge the assumptions embedded in my training and practice. This path eventually led to a growing engagement with feminist theory, psychology, and particularly social psychology. It is within this broader intellectual framework, and especially through the concept of alterity, understood not as a fixed category but as a space for ethical encounter (Freitas & Benetti, 2015) that my current work continues to find meaning.

Rather than offering definitive answers, this book serves as an invitation to return to a space of listening, reflection, and encounter. It seeks to contribute to the emotional and ethical dimensions of journalistic practice in an era increasingly shaped by artificial intelligence and technological disruption (Carlson, 2014; Diakopoulos, 2019). While the following chapters present theoretical frameworks and empirical findings in greater depth, the reflections offered here provide the foundational context from which this inquiry emerged.

By situating journalistic responses to AI within broader socio-cultural and epistemological frameworks, this study advocates for a more circular, human-centered, and critically reflective approach to technological integration in the media. Instead of framing AI adoption as a binary choice—between full resistance and unquestioned acceptance—the book introduces a third perspective: *Imperfect AI*. This concept acknowledges both the promises and limitations of artificial intelligence, while encouraging a dialogical engagement (Freire, 1970) grounded in ethical responsibility, emotional awareness, and contextual sensitivity.

The inquiry that follows is shaped by ongoing transdisciplinary conversations about journalists' well-being, professional adaptability, and the nature of ethical practice in technologically evolving environments. What remains constant throughout is a commitment to understanding journalism not only as a profession, but as a relational, emotionally situated practice shaped by, and shaping, the world in which it operates.

Carolina Escudero

References

Carlson, M. (2014). The Robotic Reporter: Automated journalism and the redefinition of labor, compositional forms, and journalistic authority. *Digital Journalism, 3*(3), 416–431. https://doi.org/10.1080/21670811.2014.976412

Diakopoulos, N. (2019). *Automating the news: How algorithms are rewriting the media*. Harvard University Press.

Freire, P. (2000). *Pedagogy of the oppressed (30th anniversary* (M. B. Ramos, Trans.). Continuum. (Original work published 1970).

Freitas, R. A. & Benetti, M. (2015). Alterity, otherness and journalism: A phenomenological perspective. *PhilArchive*. http://dx.doi.org/10.25200/BJR.v13n2.2017.989

Hochschild, A. R. (1983). *The managed heart: Commercialization of human feeling*. University of California Press.

Huxford, J. E., & Hopper, K. M. (2020). Reporting with emotion: A comparison of journalists' engagement in emotional labour across media types. *Journal of Applied Journalism & Media Studies, 9*(1), 39–60. https://doi.org/10.1386/ajms_00010_1

Ivask, S., Waschková Císařová, L., & Lon, A. (2023). "When can I get angry?" Journalists' coping strategies and emotional management in hostile situations. *Journalism, 25*(10), 2099–2116. https://doi.org/10.1177/14648849231199895 (Original work published 2024).

Kotišová, J. (2020). *Crisis reporters, emotions, and technology: An ethnography*. Springer Nature.

Kusch, R. (1976). Indios, mestizos y la cuestión nacional. [Indigenous Peoples, Mestizos, and the National Question]. Ediciones del Sol.

Lecheler, S. (2020). The emotional turn in journalism needs to be about audience perceptions: Commentary—Virtual special issue on the emotional turn. *Digital Journalism, 8*(2), 287–291. https://doi.org/10.1080/21670811.2019.1708766

Pantti, M., & Wahl-Jorgensen, K. (2021). Journalism and emotional work. *Journalism Studies, 22*(12), 1567–1573. https://doi.org/10.1080/1461670X.2021.1977168

Şahin, S. (2021). Journalism in conflict-affected societies: Professional roles and influences in Cyprus. *Media, War & Conflict, 15*(4), 553–569. https://doi.org/10.1177/1750635220987746

Stupart, R. (2021). Feeling responsible: Emotion and practical ethics in conflict journalism. *Media, War & Conflict, 14*(3), 268–281. https://doi.org/10.1177/17506352211013461 (Original work published 2021)

Acknowledgments This book would not have been possible without the active participation and the generous *oui, shì, sí, sim* and *yes* offered by journalists from diverse countries, who kindly agreed to be interviewed and to share their insights and experiences. This work is, above all, for them and made possible by them.

I express my deepest appreciation to the Global Programs Office at the University of Missouri School of Journalism particularly to Dr. Fritz Cropp for his unwavering encouragement and institutional backing throughout the course of this research. I am equally grateful to Dr. Ernest Zhang for his advice. Furthermore, I extend my heartfelt thanks to Dr. Anna Gladkova of Lomonosov Moscow State University and to Dr. Federico Rey Lennon of Universidad Católica Argentina for their generous support and valuable contributions, which were instrumental in advancing the writing of this book.

Throughout the writing process, I often found myself recalling countless conversations, reflections, and shared moments with my colleagues, journalists and editors, from whom I have learned immensely and who have remained constant figures in my personal and professional journey. To them, I extend my gratitude for their enduring presence and camaraderie.

I am also profoundly thankful to Dr. Rebecca Martínez, whose thoughtful engagement and intellectual companionship across different stages of this project transformed the writing process into an opportunity for creative exploration, personal reflection, and dialogic inquiry. I likewise wish to acknowledge Dr. Roberto Mercadillo, Universidad Autónoma Metropolitana (Mexico) whose insightful, critical, and ethically grounded perspective enriched this work in meaningful ways and offered invaluable contributions at key moments of its development.

Competing Interests The author has no competing interests to declare that are relevant to the content of this manuscript.

Contents

About the Author

Carolina Escudero Ph.D., is a lecturer at the University of Missouri and an Associate Professor in the Department of Journalism and Communication Studies at the Autonomous University of Barcelona. Her research explores international journalism, mental health, media effects, the digital divide, and social movements. She has presented her work at over 60 international conferences and has published articles and book chapters in multiple languages. Dr. Escudero is an active member of the International Association for Media and Communication Research (IAMCR) and the Latin American Studies Association (LASA); she has been recognized with various scholarships and grants, including the Leonardo da Vinci grant from the European Union and the Women and Gender Studies grant in the United States. She earned her doctoral and postdoctoral degrees in Social Psychology in Argentina, a master's degree in Sexual Difference Studies from the University of Barcelona, and a bachelor's degree in journalism from University Robert Schuman in Strasbourg, France. Before transitioning to academia, Dr. Escudero worked as a journalist and correspondent across Latin America and Europe. https://orcid.org/0000-0002-6591-9611

List of Tables

CHAPTER 1

AI in Journalism: A Transdisciplinary Approach

Abstract This study examines the emotional dimensions of journalists' experiences with the integration of artificial intelligence (AI) into media practices. Grounded in a transdisciplinary theoretical framework, the research draws on Hochschild's (1983) theory of emotional labor, Freire's (1970) critical pedagogy, and Galtung's (1996) conflict theory, alongside the ontological perspective of *ser-estando* proposed by Kusch (1976). These frameworks are complemented by contributions from emotion studies and cultural psychology, which emphasize the socially constructed and historically situated nature of emotional experience. By situating emotional labor within the context of technological disruption, the study builds upon prior research highlighting the psychological impact of rapid technological change on journalists. The qualitative approach, based on in-depth interviews with journalists from seven countries, is designed to investigate how professional identities, ethical concerns, and emotional experiences intersect in an era increasingly shaped by AI. This inquiry advocates for a human-centered and ethically attuned understanding of AI integration in journalism, emphasizing the importance of emotional awareness, critical thinking, and professional care in addressing emerging technological challenges.

Keywords Emotional labor · Journalism · Artificial intelligence · Technological disruption · Ethical responsibility · *Ser-estando*

© The Author(s), under exclusive license to Springer Nature Switzerland AG 2025

C. Escudero, *Mediating Imperfect AI*,
https://doi.org/10.1007/978-3-032-01290-6_1

Emotions are fundamental to the human condition, shaping how individuals construct meaning about themselves and navigate the environments in which they live, work, and interact. From this premise, the present study opens with a seemingly simple yet profoundly revealing question: *How do you feel about the irruption of artificial intelligence (AI) in (your) media?* This question was posed to 28 journalists from seven countries—Argentina, Brazil, China, France, Mexico, Spain, and the United States—as a way of anchoring in-depth interviews in a present emotional state. Rather than starting with technical or procedural inquiries, this emotional entry point seeks to establish a more authentic and humanized dialogue with each participant, initiating conversation from the core space where feelings and perceptions emerge.

In this regard, the concept of *ser-estando*, drawn from the philosophical work of Rodolfo Kusch (1976), serves as an epistemological anchor throughout the research. While Western philosophical traditions tend to privilege *ser*—being—as a static and universal condition, Kusch's framework offers a culturally rooted alternative. *Estar*, by contrast, reflects a dynamic, relational, and situated form of existence, deeply embedded in social, historical, and communal contexts. As Holas (2017) observes, the nuances of *estar* are difficult to translate fully into English because they carry connotations of coexistence and affectivity that transcend literal interpretation. For this reason, throughout this study, the hybrid concept *ser-estando* will be retained in its original Spanish to preserve its conceptual richness.

The central objective of this book is to explore how journalists emotionally experience and respond to the integration of artificial intelligence in their professional environments. The analysis is situated within the theoretical framework of emotional labor, as articulated by Hochschild (1983), who distinguishes between *emotions* as socially constructed performances shaped by institutional norms and *feelings* as internal, subjective states. Within this framework, emotional labor refers to the regulation and performance of emotions to meet occupational expectations—particularly in professions that require the public display of emotions that may not necessarily align with one's inner reality.

By applying this lens, the study examines how journalists confront and negotiate the affective demands prompted by the adoption of AI in their media environments. I investigate how they attempt to reconcile emerging technological norms with their own ethical convictions, professional identities, and emotional truths. In doing so, the research reveals a complex landscape of emotional negotiations—ranging from curiosity and adaptability to discomfort and resistance—which reflects broader tensions between innovation and professional integrity.

Returning to Kusch's (1976) distinction between *ser* and *estar*, this inquiry posits that journalists' responses are not only shaped by their personal attitudes toward technology but also by their embeddedness within specific socio-cultural, professional, and institutional contexts. The concept of *ser-estando* thus provides a lens through which to interpret these responses not as isolated reactions, but as situated expressions of emotional, ethical, and professional positioning. In this distinction between *ser* and *estar*, Kusch (2012) does not overlook the importance of being able to name and specify such differences, expressing that "a definable world, in turn, is a world without fear, whereas a world subject to the fluctuations of circumstance is a fearful one" (2012, p. 265). Journalists are not merely reacting to AI in the abstract; rather, they are responding and following Kusch, some are defining their experiences from their media environments.

Ultimately, this emotionally grounded approach leads us toward an ethics of relationality–toward *the Other*–in the Levinasian sense. Levinas (1969) suggests subjectivity is fundamentally shaped by an ethical encounter with the Other, where ethics originate in the face-to-face interaction. In this context, the journalist's emotional experience is not an isolated phenomenon but one that reflects their ethical responsibility and the potential impact of their profession on others. Drawing attention to those who co-constitute the journalistic profession—audiences, sources, colleagues, and communities—we can understand these relationships as embedded within the emotional experiences of journalists, underscoring the need to view AI not only through a lens of efficiency or innovation, but also through one of care, context, and ethical responsibility. Thus, in the articulation of feelings, in this *ser-estando* following Kusch (2012, p. 14) "From the emotional realm, and from its deepest layers, emerge the main foundations of a person's life" the presence of the Other cannot be excluded, as it inherently invokes ethical considerations.

Emotions shape our position and response to experiences, depending on their nature and the context in which they arise whether fear, rejection, or distrust, or conversely, joy and trust. These emotional states influence the ease or difficulty with which individuals navigate daily challenges. Various scholars have explored how *hope, purpose, and resilience* play a crucial role in overcoming extreme hardship (Frankl, 1984) and how *emotional regulation* aids in transcending adversity, particularly through problem-focused and emotion-focused coping strategies (Lazarus, 1991) and the complex interplay between emotional processes and human functioning as argue by Izard (1977, p. 4): "Emotions are fundamental to the organization of human behavior and experience, influencing perception, cognition, and action in profound ways." *Positive emotions*, such as hope and motivation, have been shown to facilitate persistence in overcoming life challenges (Dweck, 2006) and enhancing coping mechanisms and long-term well-being (Fredrickson, 2001).

Although often perceived as individual experiences, emotions are also socially constructed and historically situated. As Ahmed (2004) asserts, emotions operate as cultural practices that mediate relationships between bodies, institutions, and ideologies, shaping not only how individuals feel but also how they belong, act, and respond within specific sociopolitical contexts. As argued by Vygotsky (1978), psychological processes, including emotions, are not solely internal phenomena but are formed through social interaction and cultural mediation. This view is echoed by Martínez and Alvarado (2021), who argue that in Latin America, emotional life is deeply intertwined with communal traditions and collective political memory. Similarly, Mesquita and Frijda (1992), along with Mesquita (2001), provide compelling empirical evidence that emotions are shaped by cultural contexts and vary significantly across societies, challenging Western assumptions that emotional experiences are universal and internally contained. This cultural embeddedness of emotion is further supported by Lema (2006) and Hwang (1987), who emphasize the significance of reciprocity, interdependence, and collective identity in shaping emotional norms in Latin American and East Asian contexts. Expanding on this culturally grounded understanding, Nussbaum (2001) introduces the idea that emotions are not merely affective states but rather evaluative judgments—cognitive assessments that ascribe value and meaning to external events. From this standpoint, emotions influence not only personal well-being but also moral reasoning and civic life.

Understanding emotions as both culturally mediated and cognitively evaluative offers a valuable foundation for interpreting journalists' emotional labor. As Smith and Lazarus (1990) explain, "in considering the role of the emotions in adaptation, one must remember that the fundamental adaptational task is to mobilize the most efficacious behavior in the face of the biological and social requirements of living" (p. 612). Their cognitive-motivational theory emphasizes how emotions function as adaptive mechanisms that guide behavior in response to perceived challenges or disruptions. This theoretical lens is particularly relevant in the context of journalism, a profession increasingly shaped by technological acceleration and uncertainty.

Emotions, however, do not always align with the fast-paced emergence of new technologies, which frequently clash with the time required for reflection, as highlighted by several journalists in this study. In other words, the speed at which technological tools are created, disseminated, adopted, modified, and replaced imposes new learning rhythms that demand adaptation and acceptance. This phenomenon aligns with "technological determinism," as discussed by Adell (2006), who identifies a sequence of interconnected factors: first, technological advancements occur rapidly and continuously; second, society is expected to adapt uncritically, assuming resistance is futile. Nevertheless, Adell (2006) critiques this reasoning, arguing that it falsely assumes technological development to be an autonomous force, independent of human agency and ethical considerations. The author warns against passive acceptance of technological change, emphasizing the need for societies to critically assess and engage with these transformations rather than merely conforming to them.

Therefore, asking journalists *how they feel* at a time when a rapidly evolving technology like AI is reshaping their workflows, production processes, timelines, interactions, and prior knowledge, is both necessary and timely. This is particularly relevant in a present where the accelerated pace of technological change allows little room to pause, reflect, discern, and make sense of its uses. In this regard, perhaps this book aims to embody what Kusch suggests—a necessary pause—arriving at a moment when AI development is advancing at an unprecedented pace, so rapidly that much remains to be regulated, clarified, and integrated into journalism training programs that effectively address the needs of journalists.

Thus, in the face of this relentless technological transformation to which humanity is exposed, it is essential to keep certain fundamental questions alive: *How do I feel? How do you feel? and, if possible, how do we feel?*–as a community, as teams–so that we may understand the role of emotion in navigating this landscape of change, challenges, and uncertainties. The question itself becomes a path to one's core, exposing the normalized lack of time for introspection.

1 Overview of the Book

This book examines the complex and evolving landscape of artificial intelligence (AI) in journalism through a qualitative investigation of journalists' emotional responses to it, their experiences with technological integration, and the role of critical thinking within professional practice. At its core, the study seeks to understand how journalists interpret and navigate the challenges posed by AI while upholding ethical responsibilities in their daily work.

This research draws upon theoretical frameworks such as emotional labor (Hochschild, 1983), critical pedagogy (Freire, 1970), and the sociology of technology (Adell, 2006), in order to analyze how journalists engage affectively and cognitively with these emerging technologies. It is further enriched by Emmanuel Levinas's (1969) ethics of alterity, which emphasizes ethical responsibility in relation to the Other—be it colleagues, audiences, or those affected by journalistic work. Additionally, this work incorporates Johan Galtung's (1996) conflict theory, specifically his ABC Triangle model, to frame the tensions that emerge when AI is introduced into newsrooms. This model emphasizes three interconnected elements of conflict—Attitudes (A), Behavior (B), and Contradictions (C)—which are examined in light of journalists' emotional expressions, workplace dynamics, and structural conditions surrounding technological change. Therefore, in addition investigating journalists' affective and cognitive responses to AI, this research seeks to understand their reflections on education, ethical norms, and media practice.

This work contributes to the expanding field of journalism studies by addressing the intersection of technological innovation and emotional labor, and it advocates for culturally sensitive and context-aware strategies that support the psychological well-being of journalists, promote collaborative learning environments, and prioritize ethical literacy in the development and implementation of AI tools. Moreover, it highlights the importance of fostering critical thinking among journalists, equipping them to reflect on the implications of technological shifts while preserving the humanistic and democratic values at the core of the profession.

The structure of this publication consists of four core chapters, in addition to the Preface and Conclusion. The first chapter presents the Literature Review, focusing on the emergence of Artificial Intelligence (AI) in journalism. It examines the integration of AI training in media organizations and its impact on journalists' professional practices and emotional experiences.

The Theoretical Framework explores the adaptation and the intersection between emotions and knowledge integration in an era of rapid technological advancements. Chapter2 outlines the methodological aspects of the study, detailing the selection criteria for interviewees and the data collection procedures for the respondents from seven different countries. Chapter 3 presents the research findings, followed by Chapter 4, which provides a critical discussion of the results, interpreting the emotional and cognitive tensions associated with AI adoption in journalism. It also explores the expressed needs of journalists regarding AI education, ethical frameworks, and institutional support leading to the concluding chapter that synthesizes the key findings and offers directions for future research and policy development, emphasizing the importance of inclusive, ethically grounded, and emotionally attuned approaches to technological innovation in journalism. It introduces the concept of *Imperfect AI*—a framework proposed in this study—as a new avenue for inquiry and reflection within journalism and media scholarship, offering an alternative perspective that foregrounds ethical mediation, emotional complexity, and contextual understanding.

2 Advances in Journalism

Technology has been a foundational element of modern journalism since its inception, significantly transforming the landscape with the integration of computers into newsrooms. In the current era, technological advancements continue to reshape the communication ecosystem, presenting both opportunities and challenges within the ongoing technological revolution and training as suggested by Escudero (2024). In this evolving context, artificial intelligence (AI) facilitates machine learning, simulates human cognition and behavior, and expands cognitive capabilities (Samuel et al., 2022). The impact of AI on journalism is far-reaching, as it transforms how information is accessed, consumed, translated, verified, designed, disseminated, and interpreted. The emergence of artificial intelligence (AI) has significantly influenced journalistic routines and knowledge, reshaping the processes of news gathering, processing, production, and distribution (García-Avilés, 2019). Furthermore, AI has transformed information verification practices (Sánchez-González, 2022), where issues such as algorithmic bias and technological limitations have received increasing scholarly attention (Cardas-Răduţa, 2024; Nah et al., 2023). Ethical considerations and the demand for transparency have also become central concerns in the literature (Piasecki, 2024; Túñez-López, 2024).

Building upon these developments, AI has emerged as a dynamic and expanding field within communication studies, offering a foundation for the development and implementation of diverse media initiatives. The motivations driving its adoption are closely tied to the specific operational needs and strategic priorities of media organizations, which are themselves shaped by cultural and geopolitical contexts. In this context, AI not only enhances the discovery and presentation of news but also enables access to extensive data sets, facilitates trend analysis, and automates journalistic tasks—such as the transformation of text into video content. Moreover, it provides deeper audience insights and optimizes content distribution strategies (Marconi, 2020; Newman, 2021). For example, Manfredi-Sánchez and Ufarte-Ruiz (2020) argue that AI "allows the writing of journalistic pieces with predictable structures and formulas, which are sufficient for repetitive events of routine coverage" (p. 52). Similarly, Newman (2022) highlights the increasing focus among editors on leveraging AI for automated news writing, a shift that Salazar (2018) describes as fostering direct collaboration between journalists and machines and this aligns with the conclusion reached by Attard et al. (2023, p. 67): "As information integrity becomes more stressed by new technologies, the ability of newsrooms to keep pace with more-sophisticated attacks will require specifically created tools."

However, this collaboration is part of a broader transformation that raises debates regarding the quality and plurality of AI-generated content (Spyridou & Ioannou, 2025), alongside critical ethical concerns (Gutiérrez-Caneda et al., 2024; Sonni et al., 2024), skepticism, and caution among journalists explained in the studies conducted by Kalfeli & Angeli (2024) and Akeran et al., (2024) and in the Global South addressed by Ogola (2024). Moreover, despite these advantages, smaller news outlets often face significant challenges in adopting AI technologies due to resource constraints and structural limitations (Goleatz et al., 2018).

Given these concerns, some studies have focused on the AI regulations in the European Union governance (Pierson et al., 2024), and various ethical guidelines have begun to emerge within news organizations, yet their practical implementation remains challenging and underexplored (Porlezaa, 2023; Porlezza et al., 2024; Túñez-López et al., 2024). Sánchez-García et al. (2025) point out that these self-regulatory frameworks primarily stem from individual initiatives aimed at restricting the use of generative AI in journalistic text production. Such guidelines emphasize ethical commitments, including transparency, content verification, and respect for data and copyright. Nonetheless, Møller and Skovsgaard (2024; p.2) contend that "understanding the complex dynamics around artificial intelligence and developing a response for journalism also requires perspectives that bring us back to the level of journalistic work." Simon also emphasizes the importance of retaining a journalistic lens, noting that (2024, p. 37) "it seems increasingly clear that AI will play a transformative role in reshaping news work, from editorial to the business side."

These developments underscore the critical role of journalists not only as content producers but also as interpreters of technological change. As AI continues to permeate newsroom practices, journalists are increasingly required to understand not only how to use these tools but also how to critically assess their implications. In this context, training in the applications and limitations of AI is—and will continue to be—essential, as highlighted by various studies that examine the intersection of journalism and emerging technologies. Several scholars also emphasize the pivotal role of education in equipping media professionals with the necessary skills and ethical frameworks to lead through an AI-mediated information environment, thus pointing toward the urgent need to readdress journalism education in the digital age.

2.1 *Education on AI*

Professional training in journalism not only equips journalists with the necessary skills and knowledge to effectively perform their duties and to report the news but also influences their ability to navigate professional challenges. The integration of artificial intelligence (AI) in the media sector necessitates both substantial investment and extensive training, potentially exacerbating the existing divide between large media conglomerates and smaller, local outlets (Rinehart & Kung, 2022). In this regard, Simons (2023) argues that while artificial intelligence (AI) may not revolutionize journalism outright, it is far from a transient trend. This underscores the growing necessity for AI training among journalists—an issue also highlighted by Trattner et al. (2022), who emphasize the importance of an interdisciplinary approach that involves integrating knowledge, methods, and perspectives from two or more disciplines to advance fundamental understanding or solve problems whose solutions are beyond the scope of a single discipline (Repko and Szostak (2020). Meanwhile, Aliabadi et al. (2023) advocate for a transdisciplinary framework in AI education. This framework transcends traditional disciplinary boundaries by integrating and synthesizing knowledge across disciplines, often incorporating non-academic stakeholders in the research process and according to Lang et al., (2012, p. 27) is "a reflexive, integrative, method-driven scientific principle that aims at the solution or transition of societal problems." Given these challenges, scholars emphasize the importance of prioritizing resource allocation toward professional training to ensure the responsible adoption of AI in both newsrooms and educational environments (Tejedor et al., 2023; Sivira-Camacaro, 2025).

The significance of AI applications in higher education is particularly relevant in communication studies, as students increasingly demand more comprehensive training to meet the challenges posed by this technology (Lopezosa et al., 2023; Salvat-Martinrey et al., 2024). For example, Salazar (2018) asserts that workforce reinvention is inevitable, as journalists must be trained not only in traditional news production but also in collaborative work with AI-driven systems. This dual expertise is particularly relevant, as López-García and Vizoso (2021) observe that while media professionals and digital migrants recognize AI's potential, they often lack the necessary expertise to fully leverage its benefits. Shoai (2024) analyzes the main challenges journalists face regarding AI in their professional field in Latin America and explores the training needs and the characteristics of an educational program that could empower journalists in the region.

Furthermore, AI is reshaping epistemic standards due to its influence on professional responsibilities. In response, Lermann-Henestrosa and Kimmerle (2024) highlight the urgent need for further research and broad public debate to accompany the diffusion of AI and examine societal attitudes toward its implementation. Future research directions remain open, particularly in developing ethical guidelines and best practices for AI integration in newsrooms (Gutiérrez-Caneda et al., 2023). Additionally, the economic conditions and socio-cultural contexts of individual countries may significantly impact AI's adoption in journalism (Parrat-Fernández et al., 2024). From an educational perspective, Amponsah and Ataniashie (2024) advocate for a balanced approach to integrating AI in journalism, ensuring that technological advancements align with journalistic integrity and ethical principles.

Less is known about the feelings surrounding journalists' use of AI. One study on this emerging topic by Escudero and Zhang (2025), which emphasizes how journalists *feel* about AI rather than how they *use* it, demonstrates that journalists who possess knowledge of the tool tend to develop a sense of control. This control is expressed through increased confidence, which, in turn, contributes to greater emotional reassurance and peace of mind. Among the findings, the researchers reveal that in countries where journalists have received very little or almost no training in AI (Brazil, France, and Spain), "rejection" predominates. While in countries where journalists received training (China and Mexico), tranquility prevails. This research confirms that training in artificial intelligence (AI) generally has a positive impact on journalists, whereas the absence of such training tends to increase resistance and generate discomfort. However, journalists who reported feeling at ease with AI—either due to prior knowledge or having received training—often framed this sense of calm as a possible form of adaptation or as a strategy for maintaining their employment. This aligns with Hochschild's (1983) conceptualization of emotional labor as the management of feelings to fulfill the emotional requirements of a job. Overall, the findings indicate that many journalists who have undergone AI training expressed dissatisfaction with how these sessions were conducted, although they did not elaborate on specific shortcomings. Others noted that the training programs were primarily focused on the operational use of AI tools, without offering guidance—particularly for younger journalists—on how to avoid over-reliance on these technologies. These insights have motivated the decision to deepen the investigation through a qualitative research approach, specifically by conducting in-depth interviews to explore the emotional and professional experiences of journalists in greater detail.

2.2 *Journalists' Emotions in the Age of AI*

As emerging technologies and artificial intelligence (AI)-driven tools become increasingly integrated into journalistic practices (Posetti et al., 2021), recent studies emphasize that journalists experience a range of emotional responses to these transformations, revealing a growing need for emotional connection and regulation within the profession (Díaz-Lucerna & Vicente Fernández, 2024). Relatedly, several scholars have investigated the presence and role of emotions in journalism, contributing significantly to the understanding of journalists' emotional well-being and affective labor (Kotisová, 2019; Wahl-Jorgensen, 2019). This body of work has spanned the last few decades, exploring various emotional dynamics within journalism. Notably, much of this research focuses on the emotional toll of covering tragic events such as tsunamis, terrorist attacks, and armed conflicts, and the persistent stressors inherent in the profession (Backholm & Björkqvist, 2010; Dart Center, 2008; Stupart, 2021). These studies have provided invaluable insights into the psychological burden journalists carry, emphasizing the emotional challenges they face in high-stakes and traumatic reporting environments. In addition, scholars have delved into how the pervasive stressors of the profession affect journalists across different regions, analyzing how various factors contribute to burnout, anxiety, and moral distress (Hughes et al., 2021; Monteiro et al., 2016; Thomson, 2021).

The exploration of journalists' exposure to trauma and its emotional repercussions has gained significant traction in global research. For example, studies have examined journalists' mental health challenges in conflict zones and areas affected by natural disasters (Barnes, 2016; Buchanan & Keats, 2011; Flannery, 2022; Flores-Morales et al., 2012). These investigations have highlighted the profound psychological impacts that such exposure can have on journalists, further deepening the understanding of the profession's emotional demands. At the same time, other studies have focused on the prevalence of specific emotional disorders among journalists, such as anxiety, burnout, and technostress, all of which are exacerbated by the ever-increasing pressures of modern journalism (Escudero et al., 2023; Pantoja-Lima et al., 2022; Posetti et al., 2021). The phenomenon of moral injury, a form of psychological distress resulting from conflicts between professional duties and personal ethics, has also been explored (Feinstein et al., 2018), underscoring the complex emotional landscape journalists navigate daily.

In response to the emotional challenges faced in journalism, significant research has focused on resilience and professional values (Frazão-Nogueira & Pinto, 2024; Pearson et al., 2021), as well as the ways in which media professionals adapt their emotions to align with industry expectations (Forja-Pena, 2024; Örnebring, 2018; Wasserman, 2018;

Wharton, 2009). Meanwhile, other scholars have concentrated on identifying potential solutions and preventive measures to safeguard journalists' mental health and well-being (Deuze, 2023; Storm, 2023).

Additionally, recent scholarship has examined the role of emotional regulation in journalism and advocated for the integration of mental healthcare into journalism education. These studies propose care-oriented strategies—such as mindfulness programs, emotional resilience training, and support mechanisms—to assist journalists in managing the psychological demands inherent in their profession (Escudero et al., 2023; Escudero, 2024; Gascón et al., 2021; Pearson & Seglins, 2022; Simunjak, 2023). Such approaches aim to provide journalists with the resources necessary to preserve their emotional well-being while maintaining professional standards, thereby fostering healthier, more sustainable work environments. In parallel, Montal and Reich (2017) have argued that the development and implementation of algorithms for automated news production bring not only technological advancements but also substantial socio-political, legal, occupational, and psychological implications for journalists, news organizations, and their audiences.

Amid these evolving dynamics, an increasing body of research is now focusing on the psychological and emotional impact of artificial intelligence (AI) on journalism professionals. For instance, Upadhyay et al. (2024) conducted a large-scale quantitative study exploring the psychological effects of AI integration in newsrooms across Egypt, France, and the United Arab Emirates. Their findings revealed a notable correlation between AI-induced job insecurity and rising levels of depression among journalists. The authors emphasize that although AI may contribute to anxiety and stress, it may simultaneously reduce workload-related pressure by automating repetitive or routine tasks. Similarly, Smith and Doe (2024) examine the relationship between AI adoption and journalists' mental health, underscoring the link between perceived job instability and heightened anxiety and depressive symptoms. Their work suggests that AI functions as both a source of professional tension and a potential tool for relieving cognitive and operational burdens.

Further supporting these findings, the *Financial Times Strategies* (2025) report surveyed over 1900 employees across newsrooms in Europe, the Middle East, and Africa, identifying a prevailing sense of cautious optimism. While many respondents acknowledged AI's capacity to enhance newsroom efficiency and foster creativity, they also expressed ongoing concern regarding job security, the reliability of AI-generated content, and the ethical boundaries of algorithmic journalism. These results are consistent with the research conducted by Ayyad et al. (2024) in the United Arab Emirates, which similarly highlights the dual perspectives of opportunity and apprehension tied to AI in terms of job stability and performance metrics. Echoing this perspective, the *Thomson Reuters Foundation* (2025) reported that journalists in the Global South and other emerging economies generally approach AI with measured optimism. Although they recognize the technology's potential to streamline workflow and support content production, they also stress the pressing need for comprehensive training and ethical oversight to mitigate risks and ensure responsible use.

As previously mentioned, in addition to concerns surrounding job insecurity, the integration of artificial intelligence (AI) into journalism has been increasingly associated with elevated workplace stressors. Serrano-Oceja (2023) analyzed the psychological consequences of job precariousness within the context of AI implementation, arguing that the uncertainty generated by technological disruption—combined with the emotional burden of adapting to constantly evolving tools—calls for the development of targeted policies and specialized training programs aimed at mitigating these adverse effects. This perspective is reinforced by Cabra (2022), who found that the digital transformation of newsrooms has not only expanded journalists' professional responsibilities but has also subjected them to an ongoing cycle of adaptation. Based on surveys conducted in Canada, Spain, and Ecuador, Cabra reported that over 60% of media professionals acknowledged experiencing high levels of anxiety, with approximately one in five respondents reporting symptoms of depression. Among the key factors contributing to these psychological strains were the pressure to produce news content with greater speed and frequency, exposure to traumatic events, and the blurring of work-life boundaries exacerbated by persistent digital connectivity.

These findings underscore a complex paradox: while AI is frequently promoted as a solution for improving newsroom efficiency and productivity, its integration into journalistic practice often contributes to intensified emotional labor, increased cognitive demands, and reduced opportunities for recovery. As such, the transformation of journalistic workflows through AI requires more than technical implementation—it necessitates a critical reassessment of how emerging technologies affect the psychological health of media professionals. In this regard, Martínez-Navarro (2025) underscores "the need to integrate AI critically and consciously since it is indispensable in contemporary journalistic work to ensure the quality and integrity of news content, as well as to preserve the fundamental role of journalists" (p. 260).

Taken together, the growing body of empirical research highlights not only the emotional and professional challenges that journalists face in adapting to AI but also the urgent need for proactive interventions that prioritize mental health and well-being in the workplace. These insights suggest that responsible AI adoption must include structural safeguards and institutional support mechanisms that acknowledge the emotional realities of journalistic labor.

Against this backdrop, the present study seeks to advance and refine our understanding of journalists' emotional responses to AI in a media landscape characterized by accelerated technological innovation and systemic precarity. The convergence of emotional labor and AI integration in journalism represents a profound transformation in how news is produced, circulated, and interpreted. As such, exploring this intersection is essential to ensuring that the adoption of AI tools does not compromise journalistic integrity, emotional sustainability, or the broader democratic function of the press in contemporary society.

2.3 *Perspective of the Work*

This study, grounded in a constructivist approach, illustrates the transdisciplinary nature of emotion, demonstrating how various theoretical frameworks contribute to a comprehensive understanding of emotions in journalism. In light of this, the research problem will be approached from the perspectives of adaptation: emotional labor (Hochschild, 1983), followed by the critical perspective on adaptive processes presented by Adell (2006), Adell-Segura (2010), Freire (1970) and its intersections with ethics and the concept of *otherness* as developed by Levinas (1976), without overlooking the tensions, differences, and conflicts that these processes provoke—particularly where divergence deepens. For this reason, Galtung's (1996) perspective on conflict is also employed as a theoretical reference, specifically his Conflict Triangle Theory, also known as the ABC model (Attitude, Behavior, and Contradiction). While the model does not explicitly define "adaptation" as a core concept, the notion of adaptation is implicitly embedded within it, particularly in the ways in which individuals and groups respond to conflict and engage in processes of transformation and resolution. Through this lens, conflict is not only a site of disruption but also a potential space for negotiation, ethical engagement, and adaptive change.

Since this research focuses on emotion, I reference its etymological meaning: emotion originates from the Latin word *emotio*, which derives from *emovere*, meaning "to move out" or "to stir up" (Harré, 1986). This explanation reflects the dynamic and motivational nature of emotions, emphasizing their role in driving human behavior and responses. I adopt Hochschild's (1983) theory of emotional labor, in which the author asserts that many jobs require workers to exhibit specific emotions, often necessitating the suppression of genuine feelings in favor of those deemed appropriate for the customer or the workplace. Hochschild identifies two main types of emotional labor: Surface acting, which involves faking the desired emotions without feeling them. Employees may smile or display friendliness while internally feeling otherwise. Deep acting, in contrast, involves genuinely trying to feel the emotions one is expected to convey. In other words, the author emphasizes that workers engage in techniques to align their true feelings with the required emotions. Nevertheless, this form of adaptation in the workplace can result in a range of consequences for employees, including emotional dissonance, burnout, and feelings of alienation. These outcomes intersect with Wharton's (2009) analysis, which suggests that professionals in fields such as journalism, healthcare, and customer service engage in emotional labor as a coping mechanism to manage stress and uncertainty—thereby reinforcing its function as an adaptive strategy. This emotional toll can significantly affect workers' mental health and job satisfaction. In that sense, Hochschild argues that emotional labor represents a commodification of feelings, where genuine emotional exchanges are often replaced by scripted and commercialized displays of emotion. Specifically, Hochschild's emotional labor theory highlights the intricate relationship between work and emotional expression, shedding light on the hidden costs of service work and the pressures faced by employees.

Regarding the adaptation process involved in acquiring new knowledge—in this case, artificial intelligence—this study draws on Freire's (1970) critical pedagogy, which conceptualizes education as a process of liberation and social transformation. Freire's theory of education is centered on the idea that traditional educational systems often serve as mechanisms of oppression, maintaining existing power structures and limiting critical consciousness. In *Pedagogy of the Oppressed* (1970), the author critiques what he calls the "banking model" of education, where students are treated as passive recipients of knowledge deposited by teachers. This system, according to Freire, reinforces social hierarchies and prevents learners from developing the ability to question and transform their reality.

In contrast, Freire advocates for an emancipatory education rooted in dialogue, critical thinking, and problem-posing pedagogy. He emphasizes that education should be a collaborative process where both teachers and students learn from each other and is based on critical consciousness (*conscientização*), where individuals develop a critical understanding of their social, political, and economic reality. This process enables them to recognize and question the structures of oppression in their lives (Freire, 1970, 1974). Dialogue is essential in the educational process, as it allows educators and students to construct knowledge collaboratively. This interaction fosters an environment of respect and empathy (Freire, 1985, 1996). Praxis is also a key component and refers to the combination of reflection and action. To transform reality, educators and students must critically reflect on their experiences and act accordingly (Freire, 1976, 1998).

In other words, for Freire, education is not merely the transmission of knowledge but rather an active, dialogical process in which all participants—both educators and students—play a crucial role, making education a powerful tool for social transformation. Thus, education serves as a means of empowerment, enabling individuals to become agents of change within their communities. In the same vein, Adell-Segura, through his research, promotes a comprehensive approach to digital literacy that, like Freire, encompasses critical thinking and collaborative competencies, emphasizing the role of education in fostering active participation and social awareness. He argues that "Digital competence is not limited to the instrumental use of technologies; it also involves a critical and reflective attitude toward digital content and its influence on society" (Adell-Segura, 2010, p. 235). His contributions are grounded in a range of analogies that facilitate a clear understanding of his arguments. Adell (2011) highlights the importance of skepticism and critical evaluation of technological innovations; for instance, his "Groundhog Day" analogy and the cycle of hype, hope, and disillusionment serve as a cautionary framework against uncritical adoption of emerging technologies, encouraging a more thoughtful and measured approach to integrating technology into society. Furthermore, the "Trojan Horse" analogy functions as a critical reminder that technology should not be viewed as a neutral instrument but rather as a mechanism capable of reshaping and, at times, exerting control over social structures.

To examine the intersections between emerging technologies and emotional responses, a transdisciplinary approach drawing on sociology, pedagogy, philosophy, and cultural peace studies can be particularly illuminating. Such an approach facilitates a nuanced understanding of how journalists' emotions are shaped by their personal experiences, professional responsibilities, and the broader socio-cultural contexts in which they operate. While this book analyzes the experiences of journalists from seven countries, caution must be exercised when attempting to generalize these findings to other cultural or institutional contexts. Nevertheless, emerging evidence indicates that many of the emotional, ethical, and professional dynamics observed in this study are reflective of broader patterns within global journalism. The following chapter will elaborate on the methodological framework that guided the research design, data collection, and analytical processes employed throughout the study.

CHAPTER 2

Methodology and Procedures

Abstract This chapter details the qualitative methodological framework employed to examine journalists' emotional responses to the integration of artificial intelligence (AI) in media environments. Building upon an earlier mixed-methods study by Escudero and Zhang (2025), this research expands the inquiry through in-depth, semi-structured interviews with 28 journalists from seven countries, ensuring gender parity. The cross-national design enriches the contextual depth and supports the analysis of emotional and professional experiences. Drawing from interpretive and constructivist traditions in qualitative research (Charmaz, 2014; Denzin & Lincoln, 2018), this study emphasizes a data-driven, thematic content analysis grounded in participants' narratives. The selection of participants through purposive sampling (Bryman, 2016) and the application of cross-cultural qualitative interviewing techniques (Rubin & Rubin, 2012) ensures rigor and authenticity. Ethical considerations were prioritized, with systematic anonymization and informed consent procedures. This methodology aims to capture the nuanced affective landscapes that journalists experience in response to technological disruption, aligning with critical perspectives on emotional labor, digital transformation, and cross-cultural media research.

Keywords Qualitative methodology · Semi-structured interviews · Cross-cultural research · Emotional dynamics · AI in journalism · Thematic analysis · Media ethics

© The Author(s), under exclusive license to Springer Nature Switzerland AG 2025

C. Escudero, *Mediating Imperfect AI*,
https://doi.org/10.1007/978-3-032-01290-6_2

This chapter outlines the methodological framework employed in the present study, which seeks to deepen the understanding of journalists' emotional responses to the integration of artificial intelligence (AI) within their professional contexts. The research builds upon insights from a previous exploratory study by Escudero and Zhang (2025), which utilized a mixed-methods approach to examine journalists' emotional experiences in relation to AI education across the same countries included in the current investigation. While that initial study provided valuable foundational insights, the present research expands its analytical scope through the use of in-depth, semi-structured interviews. This qualitative approach is intended to offer a more comprehensive exploration of the emotional dimensions associated with AI adoption in journalism, emphasizing the subjective, context-specific, and often nuanced ways in which professionals engage with technological change.

For this qualitative and exploratory investigation, in-depth interviews were conducted with 28 journalists, comprising an equal gender distribution of 14 women and 14 men. The decision to ensure gender parity in the sample was informed by the recognition that gender constitutes a critical category of analysis in qualitative research. As noted by Denzin and Lincoln (2018) and Hesse-Biber (2014), gender influences multiple dimensions of the research process, including the formulation of research questions, participant selection, and the interpretation of findings. By incorporating balanced gender representation, the study aimed to capture a broader range of emotional experiences and perspectives related to the integration of artificial intelligence (AI) in journalism.

As previously noted, journalists from seven countries—Argentina, Brazil, China, France, Mexico, Spain, and the United States—participated in the study. This cross-national design enabled a dialogical exchange among professionals situated within distinct media systems, thereby enhancing the study's contextual richness and allowing for meaningful comparative analysis (Grieves, 2012). The research methodology prioritized direct engagement with participants to authentically represent their voices, aligning with Rubin and Rubin's (2012) emphasis on rapport-building as a cornerstone of qualitative interviewing. Consistent with the interpretive framework proposed by Denzin and Lincoln (2018), the study emphasized sustained interaction to access participants' subjective experiences and cultural specificities. This methodological orientation is further reinforced by Silverman (2017), who underscores the importance of grounding qualitative interpretation in the lived realities of those being studied.

The selection of countries was guided by the researcher's professional affiliations, language competencies, and access to local networks, which facilitated direct and meaningful interaction with participants. This rationale is consistent with scholars' assertions (Gobo, 2008; Patton, 2015; Saldaña & Omasta, 2018; Stake, 2005) that feasibility, access, and linguistic familiarity often influence site selection in qualitative case study research. Furthermore, the inclusion of these specific countries replicates the geographic scope of a previous related study, enabling continuity in data collection and offering comparative insights across time and context.

In line with Zhou (2008), this study addresses the ongoing need for cross-cultural research on technology adoption within journalism. It also responds to Löffelholz and Weaver's (2008) assertion that journalists and media scholars must engage in international collaboration to adequately address the evolving complexities of the field. As Reese (2008, p. 240) observes, "understanding journalism in an era of globalization means going beyond a general update of news systems and practices in various countries."

The following sections present a detailed overview of the methodological components of the study, including the research instruments, objectives, and participant profile alongside the rationale for their selection. The section on data collection and ethical adherence outlines the procedures used to contact participants, the informed consent protocols followed, and the coding strategies applied throughout the research process. Additionally, the chapter describes the data-driven approach adopted in this investigation, followed by an explanation of the semi-structured interview guide and the analytical framework employed to interpret the data.

1 Research Instruments

A literature review on the academic database Scopus, Google Scholar, and Web of Science was the starting point of research. The results were filtered using as keywords terms related to the intersection of AI and journalism and framing the search within the last ten years. In addition, the search was completed with reports elaborated by international organizations Alexander von Humboldt Institute for Internet and Society

(Goleatz et al., 2018), Financial Times Strategies (2025); Reuters Institute (Gimonport, 2023), Reporters without Borders (2023), Thomson Reuters Foundation (2025); UNESCO (Schiffrin, 2024), UE (European Council, 2024).

In addition to the theoretical foundation, this study employed a qualitative research design, as will be elaborated in the following sections, utilizing in-depth interviews with an international scope. The decision to adopt this methodology was informed by its extensive application in previous empirical research on artificial intelligence (AI) in journalism across various global contexts. In Europe, in-depth interviews have been central to studies exploring journalists' engagement with AI (Albizu-Rivas et al., 2024; Gutiérrez-Caneda et al., 2024; Kalfeli & Angeli, 2025; Noain-Sánchez, 2022; Sandoval-Martín & La-Rosa, 2018; Túñez-López et al., 2022). Similar approaches have been employed in Latin America (de-Lima-Santos & Salaverría, 2021; Méndez-Hernández et al., 2024; Pereira & Mastrella, 2022), North America (Danduran et al., 2023; Sién-Heikel et al., 2022; Wenger et al., 2024), Asia (Noor & Zafar, 2023; Partha et al., 2024; Yu & Huang, 2021; Yu et al., 2020), Africa (Adjin-Tettey et al., 2024; Makwambeni et al., 2024; Munoriyarwa, 2022), and Arab countries (Ahmad et al., 2023; AlAshry & Al-Saqaf, 2024), highlighting the method's cross-cultural relevance and adaptability.

Following the guidelines articulated by Creswell (2014), a qualitative approach was deemed particularly appropriate for this investigation, as it enables an in-depth exploration of complex and context-dependent phenomena. Qualitative methods are especially valuable when the aim is to understand how individuals interpret and make meaning of their experiences within specific social and cultural settings. In this case, the study sought to examine journalists' emotional responses and perceptions of artificial intelligence (AI) integration within media environments across diverse national and professional contexts. By privileging participants' narratives and lived experiences, the qualitative design allows for a nuanced understanding of how technological change is negotiated at both individual and institutional levels.

2 Objectives

The present study seeks to further explore the emotions journalists experience in relation to AI, examining how they feel and whether these emotions are linked to their educational background or recent training.

Additionally, this research aims to identify other potential factors influencing their emotional responses to AI, thereby updating previous findings and providing a more comprehensive understanding of the elements shaping journalists' current attitudes toward the technology.

The primary objective of this research is to explore journalists' emotions in response to the irruption and/or adoption of AI in their working spaces, with a particular focus on the impact of these tools in their work, routines and productions.

To achieve this goal, three specific objectives were established:

- O1. To analyze the emotional responses of journalists from diverse national contexts to the emergence and integration of AI in their media environments, identifying adaptive mechanisms.
- O2. To develop and gather cross-cultural evidence on journalists' perspectives regarding the applications, benefits, and limitations of AI in journalism.
- O3. To examine journalists' perceptions of AI across seven countries, analyzing the influence of key factors such as AI-related training (received vs. not received) and existing regulatory frameworks.

3 Participants

The journalists were purposively selected based on their knowledge, expertise, and/or professional experience within the media industry (Bryman, 2016). As Omona (2013) notes, purposive sampling is widely used in qualitative research because it allows the researcher to deliberately select participants capable of providing rich, relevant, and diverse insights. In this study, media professionals were chosen according to the following inclusion criteria: each participant had to be actively working in the field, have a minimum of ten years of professional experience in media, be between the ages of 28 and 65, and be employed in the country selected for the study.

Initial contact was made primarily via email. However, in some instances, scheduling an interview proved unfeasible, necessitating the identification and invitation of alternative candidates. For the purposes of this research, 70 invitations were disseminated in early January—ten per country—resulting in 39 affirmative responses.

As the interview process progressed, it was observed that by the fourth interview in each country, a point of saturation had been reached. This aligns with Urquhart's (2013, p. 194) definition of saturation as "the point in coding when you find that no new codes occur in the data. There are mounting instances of the same codes, but no new ones" and is supported by Given (2016, p. 135), who describes saturation as the stage at which "additional data do not lead to any new emergent themes." Likewise, Morse (1995, p. 148) emphasizes that "when the domain has been fully sampled –when all data have been collected– then replication of data occurs and, with this replication… the signal of saturation." Based on these criteria and theoretical foundations, this study confirmed saturation with a final sample of 28 journalists—four per country—each of whom provided both oral and written informed consent to participate in the interviews and to have their responses used for research purposes.

4 Data Collection and Ethical Adherence

As previously noted, in-depth interviews were selected as the primary research method, representing a widely used qualitative technique in the social sciences. According to Oxman (1998), interviews constitute a form of verbal interaction—whether written or oral—centered around a specific topic and guided by clearly defined objectives. In line with Guion et al. (2011), interviews aim to explore phenomena from the participants' perspectives and are particularly suited for collecting data on opinions, emotions, and lived experiences that "need to be explored in depth and in detail rather than simply reported in a word or two" (Denscombe, 2010, p. 174).

In this study, semi-structured in-depth interviews were employed to facilitate purposeful, focused conversations, fostering a dialogical space with the flexibility to explore participants' insights, emotional responses, personal interests, and educational experiences related to artificial intelligence (AI). The interview guide was organized into three sections (see Annex 1). The first section collected general demographic data, including gender, years of experience, and professional roles in the media. The second section explored emotional responses to the irruption and/or adoption of AI in journalism through prompts such as "How do you feel about AI?" followed by "Do you like AI?". The third section examined whether participants had received any formal or informal training on AI technologies.

All interviews were conducted with informed consent and audio recorded. They were subsequently transcribed using TurboScribe software (https://www.turboscribe.ai/)accessed 25 January 2025. As Eppich (2019, p. 85) notes, "to collect rich interview data, researchers must attend to key elements before, during, and after the interview." Accordingly, transcripts were manually reviewed and coded (Nowell et al., 2017) to identify and organize thematic patterns within the data.

The interviews were conducted in English, French, or Spanish, depending on the interviewee's language preference, and lasted an average of 30 minutes. Interviews were carried out via Zoom between January and February 2025. This platform was selected for its accessibility, cost-effectiveness, secure data transmission, and its increasing acceptance in qualitative research (Archibald et al., 2019).

To ensure standardization and confidentiality, all participants were anonymized using a consistent identification system based on their country and gender. The following coding system was implemented:

- Argentina Female/Male (AF1, AF2; AM1, AM2)
- Brazil Female/Male (BF1, BF2; BM1, BM2)
- China Female/Male (CF1, CF2; CM1, CM2)
- France Female/Male (FF1, FF2; FM1, FM2)
- Mexico Female/Male (MF1, MF2; MM1, MM2)
- Spain Female/Male (SF1, SF2; SM1, SM2)
- United States Female/Male (USF1, USF2; USM1, USM2)

This anonymization strategy was crucial for maintaining participants' privacy as suggested by Kaiser (2009) and Wiles et al., (2008) while ensuring a structured comparative analysis across national and gendered lines.

4.1 Data-Driven Approach

All interviews were recorded, transcribed, and analyzed using qualitative thematic content analysis, a method particularly suited for identifying patterns and recurrent themes in narrative data. To address the study's research questions, a coding scheme was developed based on emergent patterns observed during the close reading of the transcripts (Strauss & Corbin, 1990). This inductive approach is following Thomas (2006) recommendations and enabled the researcher to remain grounded in the data while generating conceptually rich categories (Elo & Kyngäs, 2008).

Following Charmaz's (2014) constructivist grounded theory methodology, the data analysis involved an iterative process of simultaneous data collection and interpretation to identify key themes and examine their interrelationships. The analytical procedure comprised three distinct stages of coding: Open coding, which involved breaking down the data into discrete parts to identify emerging concepts and significant emotional expressions; Focused coding, which refined and categorized these initial codes by identifying recurring patterns across the interviews; Axial coding, which sought to establish connections between categories and subcategories, ultimately enhancing thematic coherence and analytical depth.

This systematic approach enabled the construction of a nuanced, data-driven thematic framework following Brown and Clarke (2006) that advocates for a data-driven approach, where themes emerge from the participants' accounts. The findings presented in this study are grounded exclusively in the participants' narratives and emerged through an iterative process of analysis, independent of the researcher's preconceived assumptions or theoretical inclinations. Such methodological rigor enhances the credibility and authenticity of the insights obtained. The following chapter builds upon these analytical outcomes, offering a comprehensive overview of journalists' perspectives—disaggregated by gender and country—alongside their emotional responses to artificial intelligence (AI), the challenges they face, and the suggestions they propose. This broader analytical lens allows for a more contextually rich understanding of how journalists around the world interpret and engage with the evolving role of AI in their professional environments.

CHAPTER 3

What the Data Reveals

Abstract This chapter presents a qualitative analysis of journalists' emotional responses, perceptions, and attitudes toward the integration of artificial intelligence (AI) in media environments. Based on semi-structured interviews with 28 journalists from seven countries, the findings reveal a complex emotional landscape, ranging from enthusiasm and curiosity to discomfort, skepticism, and critical engagement. The study identifies key emotional categories and introduces two conceptual frameworks—Humanized Diagnostic Media Approach (HDMA) and Critical Transparency and Informed Disclosure (CTID)—to interpret how journalists navigate the challenges posed by AI. Participants emphasized the necessity of critical reflection, ethical education, institutional support, and the development of internal guidelines for AI usage within media organizations. Concerns about accelerated technological change, professional identity, environmental impacts, and the preservation of journalistic integrity emerged as cross-cutting themes. This analysis highlights the urgent need for a human-centered, dialogical, and ethically informed approach to AI adoption in journalism, acknowledging emotional experiences as integral to professional adaptation and technological negotiation.

Keywords Emotional adaptation · Newsroom transformation · Professional identity · Critical media literacy · Technological acceleration · Institutional regulation

© The Author(s), under exclusive license to Springer Nature Switzerland AG 2025

C. Escudero, *Mediating Imperfect AI*,
https://doi.org/10.1007/978-3-032-01290-6_3

The data analyses were guided by the following structure of interpretation. First, journalists' responses to the question "How do you feel about AI in your job?" were analyzed, followed by their reactions to the more direct question, "Do you like AI?" This initial stage aimed to explore emotional and attitudinal dimensions of AI adoption in journalistic practice. Second, the analysis focused on participants' broader perspectives regarding AI, including its perceived benefits, potential risks, and implications for professional identity and practice. Third, responses concerning training and regulatory needs were examined and systematically organized by country, enabling a comparative, cross-regional analysis of institutional and contextual differences.

The sample consisted of 28 journalists, with an equal gender distribution: 14 women (50%) and 14 men (50%) between 29 and 65 years. At the time the interviews were conducted—in January 2025—the participants held the following roles within their respective media organizations: editors ($n = 9$), reporters ($n = 11$), television content producers ($n = 4$), anchors ($n = 1$), broadcasters ($n = 2$), and photojournalists ($n = 1$).

1 Feelings About AI

When asked how they felt about the emergence and/or adoption of artificial intelligence (AI) in journalism, 22 out of the 28 interviewed journalists initially responded by sharing thoughts or evaluative opinions, rather than explicitly identifying their emotional states. However, when the question was reformulated to emphasize emotional expression, most of the participants ultimately expressed their feelings, revealing a complex and diverse emotional landscape.

The 50% of journalists—9 women and 5 men—conveyed discomfort or unease. For instance, AM1 stated, "I feel worried," a sentiment echoed by FM1, FF1, and MF1. Others shared stronger negative affective responses, such as BM1, who shared, "I feel rejection," and SM2, who stated, "I feel distrust." Some respondents expressed compound emotional reactions. FF2 remarked, "I feel extremely worried and afraid," while BF1 noted, "I feel uncomfortable and challenged." This sense of disorientation was similarly reflected in BF2's response: "I feel lost and obsolete." SF1 expressed ambivalence, stating, "I feel indifferent but also worried about its impact."

In contrast, four participants (2 female and 2 men) reported more nuanced feelings that combined curiosity with apprehension. AM2 said,

"I feel cautious and skeptical," while MF2 reflected, "Curious and at times scared." USM1 noted, "I feel cautious and curious," and USF1 explained, "I feel cautious about AI, and I am also concerned about not knowing where this AI boom will lead us." A particularly strong affective reaction was offered by AF2, who developed: "I feel negative about all of this. First, I feel discomfort and, to some extent, rejection toward this AI phenomenon. Additionally, I feel worried about how it will evolve and impact our work, roles, and the future of media production."

Notably, eight journalists (28%)—six of whom were women—expressed feelings of worry regarding artificial intelligence. Among these, three reinforced their concern by articulating an additional negative emotion, while one journalist combined their expression of worry with a concurrent positive sentiment. Conversely, other eight participants (28%)—5 men and 3 women—expressed positive emotions toward AI. For instance, AF1 stated, "I feel good; it is a helpful tool," while BM2 explained: "I feel calm, not because I have mastered AI, but because I associate it with an ongoing transformation process. Understanding that these are necessary developments that have occurred throughout history brings me peace." CM1 added, "I feel very good about AI. Sometimes I also feel fear, but in a positive way, we must use it consciously and critically." USM2 noted, "I feel good about it, knowing that it should be used in moderation," and MM2 stated, "I feel excitement; it excites me in a positive way."

Additionally, two male journalists, CM2 and MM1, admitted that they had never previously reflected on their emotions regarding AI. In response, CM2 stated: "I find it difficult to pinpoint a specific word. I think I feel challenged, and I feel good about it because it pushes me out of my comfort zone, which I see as a positive experience." In contrast, MM1 expressed: "I feel uncomfortable, out of sync. I feel as though I am falling behind because I have not yet fully understood what AI entails and its implications."

While two journalists chose to express what they do not feel about AI, rather than stating a clear stance: "I know what I don't feel—I don't feel anguish or concern" (SM2), followed by, "I feel that I am not afraid of it, but I am still figuring out what I feel." Table 1.

Table 1 Journalists' categories and characteristics

Journalist	*Years of Exp.*	*Emotions*
AF1	37	Good
AF2	26	Discouraged, rejected, worried
AM1	30	Worried
AM2	25	Cautious and Skeptical
BF1	11	Concern
BF2	10	Lost and obsolete
BM1	31	Rejection
BM2	35	Tranquility
CF1	10	Good & positive
CF2	14	Very good
CM1	20	Very good & fear
CM2	10	Challenged & Good
FF1	24	Worried
FF2	23	Worried and afraid
FM1	24	Worried
FM2	23	Fear
MF1	12	Worried
MF2	32	Curious and afraid
MM1	14	Uncomfortable, out of sync
MM2	30	Excitement
SF1	23	Indifferent & Worried
SF2	30	Worried & threatened
SM1	25	Neither anxiety nor concern
SM2	20	Distrust
USF1	20	Cautious and concerned
USF2	29	No fear, still figuring out
USM1	35	Cautious and curious
USM2	16	Good

Source Own elaboration

1.1 Do You Like AI?

Regarding whether they like or dislike AI, 19 journalists (67%) responded affirmatively, stating, "Yes, I like it." However, the 60%—11 men and six women—completed their response by using the word "but" demonstrating a nuanced perspective as "I like it, but I proceed with caution" (AF1), also echoed by USF1; "I like it, but I don't fully trust it" (CM1) presented in the following table. Table 2.

Additionally, two women expressed a different perspective beyond. USF2 stated: "I like it for specific uses, such as optimizing content, it

Table 2 "I like, but"

Participant	*Quote*
AF1 &USF1	I like it, but I proceed with caution
AM1	I like it, but I'm not convinced about how things will unfold
AM2	I like it, but I am not a techno-fan
BF1 & FF2	I like it, but I'm concerned about the lack of concrete legislation
BF2	I like it; it can be very helpful, but I do not like the idea that it will replace professionals
BM2	I like it in several aspects, but I am not an enthusiast—I am more of a skeptic
CM2	I like this new era of journalism with AI, but I do not trust the tool 100%. One of my biggest fears is that many journalists will develop a lazy attitude
CM1	I like it, but I don't fully trust it
CF2	I like it, but I know it does not consistently meet quality standards
FM2	I like it, I am not against AI, but I also find it important to maintain a critical perspective on it
SM2	I like it, but only if its uses are accompanied by deep and critical reflection
MM2	I like it for certain things, but that doesn't mean I am not afraid of how it will be used
MM1	I like it, but I believe it requires more regulation. Over time, it will no longer be a debate about whether we like it or not—It will simply become inevitable
SF1	I like knowing it exists, but I don't think we should use it excessively
BF2	I like it, but it needs better oversight
USM1	I like it, but I also recognize that the current version of AI is the worst iteration we will have

Source Own elaboration

is a huge time saver, among other benefits. Whether or not I like it is irrelevant; AI is happening, and we must adapt."

Similarly, MF2 articulated her stance as follows: "I don't dislike it. As a journalist, I cannot choose whether I like AI or not, it is something that is happening to humanity. Those who once said, 'I don't like the internet' or 'I don't like social media' failed to adapt and were left behind. Refusal to engage will only lead to exclusion."

Among the seven journalists (25%)—three women and four men—who expressed negative views (some elaborated on their concerns: "I don't like

Table 3 "Dou you like AI?" by categories

Category	*Journalists*
I like	CF1
I Don't like	AF2, BM1, FF1, FM1, SF2, SM1, USM2
I like, but	AF1, AM1, AM2, BF1, BF2, BM2, CM1, CM2, CF2, FF2, FM2, MF1, MM1, MM1, SF1, SM2, USF1, USM1
Adaptation	MF2, USF2

Source Own elaboration

it; I believe we are losing focus on journalistic production because of all this" (FM1); "No, I don't like it. I understand that I have no choice but to learn how to use it. However, I don't want an application to write for me—I want to improve my writing every day; that is my challenge" (AF2); "I do not like it; I am a pessimist, I know" (FF1); "I don't like it, and that is directly related to the absence of clear legislation" (SF2); SM1 reflected, "I don't like it; I suppose it is connected to my age and my perceptions of what constitutes 'good journalism.' One journalist, while expressing initial skepticism, left room for reconsideration: "I don't like it, but I am open to being convinced that it will ultimately be beneficial" (USM2). Table 3.

2 Cross-Cultural Evidence on Journalists' Perspectives on AI

Most respondents expressed a thoughtful perspective regarding the use of AI in media outlets. Many responses included phrases such as, "This is just the beginning" (CF1); "We are facing a great deal of uncertainty and rapid change" (MM1); "It is a tool that is improving day by day, but we cannot fully rely on it" (CM2); and "Right now, we are using the worst version of AI" (USM1).

2.1 Something New, Like in the Past

Furthermore, there was a noticeable awareness of the rapid development of AI and, in certain instances, the pressure to adopt AI technologies in newsrooms, often without sufficient time for adaptation, comprehension, or integration. In response to this, most of the interviewed journalists

(90%) acknowledged that these technologies could be highly beneficial, allowing them to focus on writing, conduct more in-depth investigations, and interview a greater number of sources, as the time-consuming task of transcribing interviews is significantly reduced.

The ongoing advancement of AI and its increasing influence in the media industry was acknowledged by all journalists. However, this is where perspectives diverged: 20% of respondents believed AI would bring about significant changes and job displacement, while 80% adopted a more analytical and reflective stance, arguing that this is not the first time journalism has faced technological transformation, recalling past disruptions such as the introduction of computers, the Internet, and social media.

Those who expressed concerns included statements such as, "Many colleagues could lose their jobs" (BM1) and "Over time, editors could be replaced, which would be a serious mistake" (FF1, also mentioned by AF2). In response to these concerns, SM2 argued: "If this is not regulated, it will lead to greater job insecurity in journalism and lower-quality productions. Anything can happen, and much of it depends on the regulations that are put in place."

Nevertheless, the remaining professionals shared perspectives often based on personal experiences, allowing them to contextualize the current developments within a historical framework: "It reminds me of the arrival of the Internet—everything that was said and speculated about journalism at the time. Every new technology brings doubts and discomforts that gradually diminish over time" (AF1). This retrospective perspective was echoed by AM1 and BF1 and further expanded by BM1: "Although we do not yet know the full consequences, this is an inevitable process of change, much like what happened with the introduction of computers, the Internet, social media, and other technological innovations."

According to AM2 "The impact of the Internet was profound; in contrast, AI seems more like a passing trend, similar to many other technological advancements", followed by SF2 "It is like the Industrial Revolution—it changes the way we produce, think, and even how we organize our schedules." BF2 stated, "It can be very helpful. AI saves time; we simply need to better understand its limitations and biases." In line with this, CM2 emphasized: "It is a tool, and we must be clear that it is not meant to replace our work. AI cannot do the job of a reporter—going out to cover an event, talking to people, and understanding what is happening"; CM1 added that AI "helps improve efficiency and competitiveness"; "It allows us to access more tools to enhance our work" (CF2); "AI is structured like a tree—it does not function like a human. I am not going to respond like an algorithm" (USM1). FM1 further noted: "AI will benefit journalism in some ways, but not in all, just as has happened with technological advancements in the past. However, I am also certain that AI cannot replace the in-person connection and trust we establish with our sources."

Along these lines, MM1 stated: "AI is a tool that enhances our work, not a replacement it amplifies our investigative capabilities. Our writing style will always be our own" and this aligns with AM1's perspective: "AI is a resource. I believe it is currently being overemphasized, but over time, we will realize that it cannot replace strong writing or analytical skills. It is just a matter of time." USF1 also acknowledged: "There are ways we can optimize content—it is a huge time saver. This is just another new technology. However, it is important to emphasize the necessity of using these tools ethically and responsibly."

Three of the four Spanish journalists provided a distinctive perspective on AI usage, differing from the rest of the respondents in the types of examples they used to illustrate their views. SM2 and SF2 compared AI to a kitchen knife, explaining that although its intended purpose is to aid in cooking, the same tool could be misused to cause harm. Meanwhile, SM1 compared AI to the early days of automobiles:

> When people first started driving, they didn't know how to handle cars properly. They bought them, crashed them, and caused disasters. Eventually, regulations, education, and road signs were introduced to manage traffic safely. AI seems to be in the same situation as those first cars—it requires education on its use, regulation, and restrictions on its harmful aspects.

According to FM2 that technological development follows an exponential, rather than linear, trajectory and observes, "The time required for major innovations has drastically shortened: whereas in the past, they could take centuries or decades, today they can develop within months or even weeks." This perspective highlights the accelerated pace of change in the digital era and underscores the urgency with which journalism and related fields must adapt to emerging technologies. Many of the journalists emphasized their professional competencies, such as having a strong "nose" for news and effective strategies for producing content (MF1), highlighting the conviction that "the human approach is crucial for a good story" (AF2). This perspective reinforces the argument that artificial intelligence (AI) cannot "replace" (FM1; SM1), "describe" (SM1), or effectively "angle" (CF1) news stories, as such tasks demand "empathy" (SM2), a specific "feeling" (FM1), and a deep "cultural appropriation" (MM2).

A recurring concern among participants relates to the limitations of artificial intelligence in replicating the nuanced, human-centered aspects of journalistic practice. Ten journalists (35%)—seven men and three women—emphasized that AI lacks the capacity to produce "in-depth reports" (MM2), particularly in investigative contexts "where there is more to investigate." As AM1 elaborates, "this ability to evaluate a situation and decide to change the angle or go further with one of the interviewees is connected to our journalist instinct to read between the lines and connect with our sources." FM1 similarly argues, "A machine will not replace good journalistic practices, or the connection established during interviews." This perspective resonates with SM1's detailed reflection: "A tool will never be able to describe how that match was experienced from the stadium stands—the conversations among supporters, the smells, the rhythm of the chants, the reactions to the players. That human aspect is irreplaceable." Reinforcing this sentiment, SM1 further affirms, "AI can't develop empathy during interviews or know if there is more to investigate." Ten journalists (35%)—seven men and 3 women—further noted that AI lacks the capacity to produce "in-depth reports" (MM2), especially in contexts "where there is more to investigate." As AM1 explains, "this ability to evaluate a situation and decide to change the angle or go further with one of the interviewees is connected to our journalist instinct to read between the lines and connect with our sources."

MM2 reflects on the broader context of change:

> This is a transformation. People have always talked about the end of journalism since I studied journalism. Yet, journalism continues to evolve. Even though an enormous amount of content is uploaded and updated online every day, we have to ask ourselves: Who doesn't like seeing themselves published in a printed newspaper? It still has an impact, and at the same time, it creates historical and archival material something that cannot simply be erased. Columns, analyses, and in-depth reports still require humans; they demand that essential cultural appropriation.

The idea of transformation is also underscored by BM2, who describes the current moment as "a process of transformation—these are necessary processes, and they happen." MF2 echoes this sentiment: "In response to these technological transformations, journalists have continuously adapted." Similarly, CF1 notes that although there is anxiety among Chinese journalists about job displacement, the reality points to a "transformation of roles," wherein "AI can assist with editing, but a human editor will always be needed to review, angle, and improve journalistic productions. A reporter will always be sent to cover an event."

2.2 *AI at High Speed*

The issues of speed, adaptation, and knowledge integration were explored by several journalists. AF2 remarked, "At times, I feel like I'm missing the train." Similarly, MF2 expressed, "This high-speed technology train is moving too fast, and at times, keeping up with its pace can be painful and challenging because there is no time to fully understand or grasp everything that is happening and changing." This sentiment aligns with SM1, who stated, "AI can also be perceived as a high-speed train that does not give you time to board or develop the necessary critical perspective."

BF2 echoed these concerns: "This is moving so fast that all my knowledge and experience will soon be insufficient." Likewise, BM1 reflected, "At times, it is frustrating to see that what you have just learned, which took time to understand and master, is already obsolete because each day brings a new tool that we do not have time to process." FF1 added, "This accelerated AI progress deeply concerns me."

MF1 acknowledged the inevitability of AI's rapid advancement, stating, "We are not going to stop everything AI brings or change its pace, so we must find ways to work with it while maintaining our critical perspective. We do not have to accept all of this unconditionally, without questioning or doubting." SF2 reinforced this perspective: "AI, like past technological advancements, does not wait. It progresses, it does not stop—I insist, it does not wait for us." SM2 emphasized, "The high speed of all this does not allow us time to engage in critical reflection or to analyze its impact thoroughly." In this regard, FM2 framed the issue within a broader context, characterizing it as exponential rather than linear progress: "We are witnessing an acceleration of progress. In the past, innovations could take humanity centuries or decades, whereas today, they develop within months or weeks. As technology advances faster, so does science, among other fields." SF2 concluded with a pragmatic stance: "These are not times in which journalists can afford to reject AI. We must be cautious and strive to better understand this AI boom."

2.3 Routines and Roles

A recurring theme across interviews was the significant transformation of journalistic routines and the expansion of professional roles due to technological integration, particularly in broadcast media. USM2 reflected on the reduction of team structures in audiovisual production:

> In the past, a recording team consisted of at least three people; today, just one person handles it. The quality is not the same, but this is where we are now—teams have been reduced, and this trend will continue. That is why regulation must be implemented as soon as possible.

This evolution in newsroom dynamics was echoed by FM2, who provided a detailed comparison between past and present practices:

> Going out to report for TV used to be a team effort. Back when I studied journalism, each of us had a specific role: the cameraman, the presenter, the producer, and the editor. Today, one person handles all these tasks, not to mention they also have to upload the report online, find the right keywords, and post a summary on social media. The industry has changed, and journalists have taken on many more roles.

AF2 similarly emphasized the growing demands placed on individual journalists:

> I have to do a ton of things that would have been unimaginable ten years ago. I upload my article to the media outlet's website, find the right keywords, upload images, format the text, and highlight key points. Then, I share it on social media. We are constantly being asked to do more, we are like hamsters on a wheel that never stops spinning.

This notion of overextension was reinforced by SF1, who remarked:

"We do not just write and verify sources; we also design, promote our news pieces, and upload them in multiple formats. Even though we have more tools, we end up doing more work." BF2 offered a particularly poignant reflection on the toll of these expanding expectations:

> My colleagues and I are so exhausted, so overwhelmed, that we can't see beyond the daily routine we are trapped in. When we go out to cover a story, we have to handle the interviews, video recording, audio for radio, images for the website, as well as visuals and text for social media. We do all of this knowing that our media employers are primarily focused on cutting costs, and they make that clear to us every day. They are already testing a robot as a news anchor at my workplace; I know how this story ends.

It is noteworthy that among the five journalists who expressed the highest levels of concern regarding changes to work routines and the reduction in staffing, four were employed in the broadcast sector. This finding suggests that role compression and workload intensification are especially pronounced in audiovisual journalism, where technological tools have not necessarily translated into reduced effort but rather into broader responsibilities under increasing pressure.

3 AI Training and Regulations Per Country

This section presents a country-by-country analysis to facilitate a more nuanced understanding of the perspectives shared by journalists across the seven participating nations. By disaggregating the data geographically, the analysis highlights the distinct characteristics, contextual challenges, and specific needs articulated by participants within their respective regulatory and professional environments.

3.1 *Argentina*

In Argentina, the journalists interviewed—AF1 (26 years of experience), AF2 (37 years), AM1 (30 years), and AM2 (25 years)—reported not having received formal training in artificial intelligence (AI) within their media organizations. AF2 noted, "In my case, it was my son who taught me how to use an app to transcribe audio; the newspaper hasn't provided any training to the reporters." Similarly, AF1 shared, "I haven't received any training, and I would really like to." AM1 explained, "I've been self-educating, looking for options to transcribe and verify information." Meanwhile, AM2 confirmed the absence of formal instruction and mentioned having briefly experimented with ChatGPT, which they found to be of low quality.

Despite varying levels of informal engagement with AI tools, all four journalists emphasized the urgency of structured training for media professionals. They collectively underscored the importance of addressing key ethical, technical, and regulatory aspects. AF1 emphasized: "What we don't understand becomes a threat. Media professionals must play an active role in AI's use and regulation. It is crucial to implement AI education tailored to our needs while maintaining a critical and constructive perspective." AF2 argued: "AI education should be accessible to all journalists, regardless of our section or personal interest in it. Once we are informed, we can choose whether to use it or not."

AM1 reinforced this view, stating, "Journalists must receive training, but these programs should be designed from a transdisciplinary perspective to ensure a respectful and meaningful contribution. There should be dialogue between technology experts, news producers, and editors, fostering critical analysis. Journalists and editors should not depend on AI. On the contrary, we need to be well-versed in its biases; only by understanding it thoroughly can we avoid over-reliance." AM2 further added that training should include a "critical perspective on these tools."

3.2 *Brazil*

In Brazil, none of the journalists consulted—BF1 (10 years of experience), BF2 (9 years), BM1 (22 years), and BM2 (36 years)—had received artificial intelligence (AI) training within their respective media organizations. However, some had participated in workshops organized by press associations or engaged in independent learning. BF1 recalled, "I received an offer for a course, and I signed up. It was quite general, but I'm keeping an eye out for new training opportunities." Similarly, BM1 acknowledged the absence of formal training within their organization and emphasized the need for institutional support: "It would be beneficial to have training opportunities in our workplaces. If media outlets lack the resources for training, they should collaborate with public universities so that AI education is not limited to those who can afford it." BM2 also confirmed the absence of formal training but noted:

> "My doctoral thesis was on AI in journalism, so I feel prepared for what is happening. It's not just about learning how to use the tools; I understand the broader implications and recognize the need to integrate new knowledge in this technological field."

In contrast, BF2 expressed skepticism regarding institutional commitment to professional development in this area: "I don't think it will happen. I don't believe media executives care about training us in this area. That's why I have taken the initiative to educate myself through YouTube, updating my knowledge to stay relevant in the industry."

Regarding suggestions and recommendations for future AI training, BF1 emphasized the role of governments, stating, "Governments should promote AI training while simultaneously implementing legislation that ensures responsible usage and limitations." However, BM1 offered a contrasting perspective: "I do not trust the decisions a government might make regarding AI legislation. If we have a far-right government, I worry about what they might decide. Each media organization should take responsibility for training its employees."

BM2 identified key elements that should be included in media training programs, explaining:

> Training should begin with a diagnostic study to assess journalists' needs, which would help guide technology teams in selecting the right tools and solutions. Reviewing production processes could be crucial both the journalistic and technological sectors should be involved in the training process.

3.3 *China*

In countries such as China, artificial intelligence (AI) training is commonly offered within media organizations, although it is typically not mandatory and instead presented as an optional opportunity. Among the interviewed participants—CF1 (20 years of experience), CF2 (9 years), CM1 (20 years), and CM2 (14 years)—CM1 observed that, "Even though it is optional, most people choose to participate because it allows them to better understand new tools." Similarly, CF1 affirmed the value of institutional support, stating, "The training sessions provided by media organizations are incredibly helpful, " and further emphasized, "We know there is still much to learn because everything is constantly evolving."

Also, CF2 observed, "Younger journalists are generally more curious and motivated to continue learning, whereas for older generations, it's a mindset issue—it may or may not change over time." CM2 stated that they have participated in AI training and plan to continue updating their knowledge while emphasizing the importance of maintaining a strong connection with interviewees and audiences.

Regarding future AI training, all four journalists consulted agreed that such programs help media professionals become familiar with available tools, test them, and decide whether to continue using them or explore alternatives. CF2, CM1, and CM2 also concurred that making training optional allows employees to choose when to participate and to specialize in areas that align with their professional interests or enhance their work.

However, CM2 suggested that training programs should explicitly address AI's limitations: "Young journalists must understand that AI will not do their work for them. They should not place blind trust in new tools but rather test them, critically assess their effectiveness, and discard them when necessary."

3.4 *France*

In the case of France, among the interviewed journalists—FF1 and FM1, each with 24 years of experience, and FF2 and FM2, each with 23 years—two reported having received training in artificial intelligence (AI), while the other two had not. FM1 explains:

> "I received training, and I find it uncomfortable. It reinforced my belief that there is no dialogue between the technology department and the

editorial team regarding whether certain applications are necessary and, if so, for what purpose they will be implemented. Instead, it feels like an imposition. I get the impression that journalists have no say in the matter, and that is wrong".

Similarly, FM2 confirms having received training but emphasizes his proactive approach to self-education. Reflecting on the introduction of bots in his newsroom, he observes that many reporters "rely too much on the application, to the point where they don't even double-check it." This situation, according to FM2, forces editors to not only correct journalists' mistakes but also identify errors made by AI tools. He adds: "I've noticed that it's mainly younger journalists who put too much trust in these tools." The two female journalists interviewed had not received AI training. FF1 shares: "I haven't received any training so far, but I know that other departments have. I understand that training will gradually be expanded." Meanwhile, FF2, with 23 years of experience asserts: "I have not received training, and I hope the government will begin implementing the necessary regulations and oversight. I believe this is the most important step in addressing misinformation and recognizing AI biases." Regarding recommendations for AI training in media organizations, the French journalists emphasized the need for a more active role for journalists in the training process. FM1 stated: "Journalists, as knowledge gatekeepers, should play a more active role in AI training. We should be consulted and given opportunities to engage in dialogue with technology teams." FM2 suggests that training should be carefully designed to address issues such as misinformation: "We must ensure that future generations receive proper training in these areas." FF2 advocates for a structured training program, stating: "A formal training plan for journalists is essential. We need to be able to recognize false news easily and assess AI usage from a professional and ethical standpoint. This must happen soon, as we risk losing credibility." FF1 further highlights the need for widespread AI education, proposing that AI training should be provided to all stakeholders—journalists, editors, directors, and even readers—to explain both its effects on media and society, "an ideal education model would be based on constructive dialogue, though I recognize that in large media corporations, this balance is often lacking."

3.5 *Mexico*

In Mexico, among the four journalists interviewed—MF1 (11 years of experience), MF2 (31 years), MM1 (14 years), and MM2 (30 years)—only one had received any formal training related to artificial intelligence (AI). MF1 noted: "Only the design team has received training, which was subsidized by the media outlet. They use AI through a specific program installed on one of the newsroom's computers."

MM1, with 14 years of experience, expresses concerns about Mexico lagging in AI adoption and remains on the lookout for training opportunities. Similarly, MF2, with 32 years of experience, has independently explored AI applications and the capabilities of ChatGPT. MM2, with 30 years of experience, is the only journalist to have received AI training from his media organization. He explains:

> "One of the executives made it clear during the training that it wasn't about relying on the tool but understanding it as a complement. However, younger generations tend to believe that these tools can do everything, and that's not true. The machine can produce content, but it creates a cold article—it cannot delve deeper."

In addition, the Mexican journalists believe that AI training for media professionals should acknowledge the country's relative delay in adoption while emphasizing ethical considerations. MM1 states: "We may be behind, but AI training should prioritize ethical considerations—understanding when and how to use these tools, among other factors." MF1 highlights the importance of continuous updates in AI courses, arguing that: "These courses should be regularly updated, and all media professionals should have access to them to learn how to detect fake news and understand AI biases."

MF2 underscores the need for a more human-centered approach to AI training, suggesting that it should also focus on the "heart and mind" of journalists. Meanwhile, MM2 stresses the importance of dedicating sufficient time to training—despite time constraints in journalism—and ensuring that sessions are conducted appropriately and asserts: "Training should be comprehensive, which is challenging in journalism. It must be delivered properly, uphold ethical standards, and reinforce the idea that AI is a complementary tool rather than a replacement for journalists."

3.6 *Spain*

In Spain, the four journalists interviewed—SM1 and SF2 (each with 30 years of experience), SF1 (23 years), and SM2 (20 years)—reported that they had not received any formal training in artificial intelligence (AI). When reflecting on how AI training should be implemented, SM1 emphasized the importance of voluntary participation, stating, "Journalists should have the option to choose whether or not they want to participate in training; it should be optional. However, I am aware that this will ultimately depend on the company's policies." SF2 underscored the necessity of equipping journalists with knowledge about the limitations and inherent biases of AI technologies, asserting, "The limitations of AI tools and their biases must be made clear; as journalists, we must be responsible for carrying out ethical, responsible, and honest work for both ourselves and our audience." SM2 emphasized that artificial intelligence (AI) training should account for multiple factors and be grounded in a thorough needs assessment and argued:

> "Training should begin with a diagnostic study. We need to ask: What do journalists actually need? What humanistic and social criteria should be considered in these trainings? These analyses must not be influenced by technology itself solutions should not be presented before the problem is fully understood. Right now, non-urgent needs are being imposed on us. Training programs should be developed and evaluated by institutions such as professional associations, journalists' unions, and regulatory bodies."

This perspective underscores the importance of aligning training content with the actual professional, ethical, and social needs of journalists, rather than allowing it to be driven by technological imperatives alone. SF2 proposes that one way to emphasize the importance and benefits of AI training is through media coverage. She suggests that media outlets could publish news articles and opinion columns written by their in-house technology experts to explain the value of AI training. She notes that some Spanish media outlets are already implementing this approach: "There should be a published article that both readers and journalists can access, explaining why the adoption of certain AI tools will benefit the media. This would provide a clear and positive perspective on the topic."

3.7 *United States*

In the United States, among the four journalists interviewed—USF1 (29 years of experience), USF2 (20 years), USM1 (30 years), and USM2 (10 years)—only one was actively undergoing training in artificial intelligence (AI) at the time of the interview. This journalist noted that the purpose of the training was to develop a deeper understanding of AI's applications, limitations, and implications, stating, "At the moment, everything seems to be related to AI." All four participants confirmed that they had engaged with AI in their work and were familiar with a variety of tools and applications. USM2 remarked, "I search for information and recommendations online, and I also take into account the suggestions of my colleagues who have received training or are using certain tools that they find beneficial."

Participants emphasized that AI training for journalists should be implemented through a progressive and flexible plan—one that avoids imposing additional burdens or framing the adoption of new tools as a productivity mandate. Instead, training should allow journalists the autonomy to select tools according to their individual and organizational needs. USF2 explained:

> The training should be presented as a progressive implementation plan, one that does not become a burden for journalists or an obligation to incorporate more tools. Instead, journalists should have the freedom to choose which tools they prefer to use. It should not be thought of as a productivity demand. And it should not focus solely on the technical aspects but also on the ethical considerations.

USM1 added a cautionary note, stating, "Today AI is like a black box, and the AI we are using today is the worst." Similarly, USF1 emphasized the need for thoughtful application, remarking, "We need to promote a careful, intelligent use that understands its scope, without losing sight of its environmental impact." Echoing this environmental concern, USF2 expressed support for a more ecologically conscious approach to AI integration. In addition, USM2 stressed the importance of interactive learning environments that foster engagement, suggesting, "The training should be a true learning experience, making it more interactive, allowing journalists to raise their doubts and ask questions; this way, it will be successful."

For USF1, it was essential to distinguish AI use as more than a technical skill, advocating for a reflective and critical framework: "The training should be based on critical thinking and begin with a diagnostic approach that assesses the needs of the media to move forward from a problem-solving perspective." This participant further asserted:

> The tool-first mentality doesn't make any sense; it is unfortunate and unsustainable. It should be, 'What problems can we solve? What tools are available and sustainable?' AI training should be presented as an opportunity (...) Instead of seeing it as a magical thing we do not understand, [we should focus on] how we engage with technology, how we engage with new technology. Training journalists to be curious, open-minded, and critical is essential.

It is observed that four journalists–BM2, FM1, SM2, and USF1—agree on the necessity of conducting a needs assessment for journalists before incorporating training or new tools. In this regard, the professionals argue that it is neither possible nor realistic to offer a solution to a problem that has not been clearly identified. As USF1 indicates, "These consultations should be conducted at the base of the pyramid, with the journalists," a point reinforced by SM2, who adds:

> "We must humanize these decisions, give journalists a voice, understand what they need, and why they believe it is a priority. A diagnosis should be developed, which will need to integrate other factors, before deciding what is truly a priority and what will improve journalistic work and the connection with the audience."

In addition, six journalists—AM2, BM1, CM2, FM2, MM2, and SF2—agree on the importance of explaining to new generations, with some emphasizing journalism students, that they should not blindly trust the tools. Furthermore, twelve journalists (AF1, AM1, AM2, BM1, BF2, CM2, FM2, FF2, MF1, SM1, SM2, and USF1) emphasized the need to disclose the biases and limitations of these tools. In other words, they argue that this should be a key part of AI education, both in media outlets and universities.

4 Future Directions

As a corollary to training in journalism and the use of AI, the lack of a guide and the absence of clear legislation regarding AI use in the media were discussed in the interviews. The researcher asked the journalists whether the creation of a document, such as a guide, protocol, or handbook, for AI usage by each media outlet could be helpful. Except for two journalists (BM2 and FF2), who considered that "the creation of a protocol should not be solely created within each media outlet but should respond to national legislation" (BM2), followed by "I hope to know the government's position to then move forward with internal documents" (FF2), the remaining 26 journalists agreed that each media outlet should work toward creating an internal document that clearly, concisely, and simply establishes "the uses of AI and when to consult an editor" (BF1), with the ability to "edit and update as necessary" (CF2).

AF1 stated, "I would feel much more at ease with an internal protocol guiding us in the use of AI." This sentiment of reassurance was echoed by three other interviewees—MF1, BF1, and BF2. Regarding this document, SM2 suggested that "It would be beneficial for journalist associations and unions to actively participate to add their voices and recommendations," while AF2 argued that "this would allow readers to see and recognize when AI has been used." SM1 stressed the importance of incorporating "ethical criteria for its use and recognizing its limitations and biases," and SF1 emphasized that "the values of journalism should not be overlooked." USF1 stated that the protocol should be "subject to continuous development and updates, specifying what is allowed and what is not, where the tools used should be disclosed to the audience," while MM1 proposed that the protocol should "clarify that AI tools are meant as support tools." AF2 further suggested that "journalists and different teams should participate in drafting the document, making it a collaborative effort," while not losing sight of the audience. USF2 added, "A consultation could be extended to ask readers how they feel and what they think about the media's use of AI."

4.1 Environmental Impact

Among the 28 journalists interviewed, only four women—two from the United States and two from Spain—expressed concerns about the environmental impact associated with the use of AI. SF1 stated, "I have used Google's Gemini a little, but I stopped due to its negative environmental impact; it consumes a significant amount of water, among other issues." Similarly, SF2 acknowledged the broader implications of technological advancements, noting, "Like every major revolution humanity has experienced, AI has its imperfections. The issue of pollution and its environmental impact will become more evident over time, and regulations will need to be established."

USF1 echoed these concerns, arguing, "I worry a lot about AI biases, but also about its environmental impact. We store vast amounts of information in the cloud, which has massive ecological consequences. Every time I use AI, I become more aware of the resources I am consuming." She further explained how this awareness makes it difficult for her to engage with AI tools. This perspective was also supported by USF2, who expressed a keen awareness of AI's environmental impact and emphasized the importance of education and public consciousness regarding the broader ramifications of its use. Based on the responses, two categories were developed to represent the journalists' feelings, perceptions, and needs expressed by journalists:

HDMA (Humanized Diagnostic Media Approach): this category is aligned with journalists who do not exhibit significant signs of emotional labor and who express their concerns and fears openly from a critical, conscious, and engaged perspective. These media professionals advocate for conducting a thorough needs assessment among journalists before the introduction of new tools or training initiatives. Their position asserts that any intervention must be rooted in a clear understanding of the unique challenges and experiences that journalists face. By prioritizing diagnostic assessments, this group underscores the importance of recognizing the specific contexts and lived realities of journalists, thereby ensuring that proposed solutions are both relevant and ethically sound.

CTID (Critical Transparency and Informed Disclosure): this category comprises media professionals who emphasize the necessity of disclosing the biases and limitations inherent in new technological tools. They contend that transparency should serve as a fundamental component of AI education in both media outlets and academic settings. Their argument centers on the ethical imperative to inform emerging journalists—particularly journalism students—about the potential pitfalls of relying on these tools without critical scrutiny. Drawing on Levinas's ethical framework, this position honors the "otherness" of both journalists and the technologies they utilize, advocating for a reflective and informed approach that upholds journalistic integrity and autonomy (Levinas, 1969).

As a foundation for the theoretical discussion that follows, it is essential to acknowledge that both the HDMA and CTID categories reflect a collective effort among journalists to reclaim agency within an evolving technological landscape. Rather than accepting AI implementation as a unilateral or inevitable process, these frameworks reveal an emergent call for participatory, ethically informed, and culturally sensitive modes of integration. Together, they challenge binary framings of AI as simply positive or negative, advocating instead for a nuanced, dialogical mediation that prioritizes journalistic well-being, professional responsibility, and structural transformation. These positions underscore the need to rethink AI adoption in journalism not only as a technological issue but as a socio-emotional and epistemological negotiation—one that demands reflexivity, care, and institutional accountability. The discussion that follows will further analyze how these insights align with and contribute to broader theoretical frameworks on emotional labor, ethics, and peace-oriented mediation, particularly in the context of what this study defines as Imperfect AI.

CHAPTER 4

Discussing Journalists' Feelings and Needs

Abstract This chapter offers a critical discussion of journalists' emotional responses, ethical concerns, and educational needs in the context of artificial intelligence (AI) integration within journalism. Organized into three sections—emotional responses, cross-cultural perspectives, and ethics and training—the analysis reveals complex patterns of emotional labor, professional adaptation, and ethical reflection across seven countries. While journalists express a spectrum of emotions ranging from enthusiasm to anxiety, their collective narratives emphasize the urgent need for critical AI education, transparent regulatory frameworks, and participatory dialogue within media organizations. The chapter introduces the conceptual frameworks of Humanized Diagnostic Media Approach (HDMA) and Critical Transparency and Informed Disclosure (CTID) to explain journalists' needs for ethical AI integration. It also proposes the notion of "Imperfect AI" as a way to conceptualize AI adoption not as a seamless technological shift but as a dynamic and ethically contingent process that demands continual negotiation between technological innovation, professional identity, and social responsibility.

Keywords Emotions in journalism · Critical AI education · Dialogue · Human · Centered technology · Imperfect AI · Contradictions

© The Author(s), under exclusive license to Springer Nature Switzerland AG 2025
C. Escudero, *Mediating Imperfect AI*,
https://doi.org/10.1007/978-3-032-01290-6_4

The integration of artificial intelligence (AI) into the field of journalism has elicited a wide spectrum of emotional responses, underscoring the complexity and challenges associated with emerging technologies. As discussed in previous chapters, journalists' experiences with AI are shaped not only by its technical affordances but also by the ethical, cultural, and institutional contexts in which it is implemented. This chapter is organized into three key discussion sections that reflect the multifaceted nature of these findings.

The first section analyzes journalists' Emotional responses to AI—including positive, negative, mixed, and nuanced reactions—while also exploring how professionals are adapting to technological change. These responses are interpreted through the lens of emotional labor (Hochschild, 1983), offering insight into how journalists negotiate their internal emotions in relation to external professional expectations. The second section presents cross-cultural perspectives on AI, comparing journalists' views across the seven countries studied. These accounts are placed in dialogue with the theoretical frameworks and literature reviewed earlier in the book, allowing for a more balanced and context-sensitive understanding of how AI is perceived globally. Finally, the third section focuses on ethics and training, examining what journalists consider most urgent or essential in relation to AI education. This section expands the discussion beyond technical skills to include the creation of dialogical spaces, sites where journalists, educators, and technology departments can collaboratively reflect on the implications of AI. These discussions echo the arguments presented in Chapter 1, reinforcing the need for transdisciplinary, ethically grounded, and participatory approaches to AI integration in journalism.

1 Emotional Responses

The interviews revealed a composite of emotional states—including worry, curiosity, excitement, caution, and optimism—as journalists attempt to understand and respond to the implications of AI for their profession. These responses underscore the multifaceted nature of AI's impact, suggesting that emotional reactions are shaped not only by the technology itself but also by broader socio-professional and institutional contexts.

Expressions of worry were dominant and confirmed by eight journalists (six women and two men), a reaction that may be understood through the lens of Hochschild's (1983) concept of *emotional labor*, particularly regarding the management and articulation of workplace emotions. Statements such as "I feel worried" (AM1, FM1, FF1, MF1) and "I feel extremely worried and afraid" (FF2) suggest a setting where emotional labor is less restricted, allowing genuine emotions to surface. Unlike roles in which emotional detachment is often required like in journalism appears to offer a space where vulnerability and professional concern can coexist (Piasecki et al., 2024).

This transparency may also reflect a form of *collective emotional labor*, in which journalists, as a professional group, experience shared anxieties and industry-wide disruptions (Lünenborg & Medeiros, 2020; Möller et al., 2024b). Uncertainty regarding job security and evolving editorial norms, particularly as described by Serrano-Oceja (2023), compounds the emotional burden. These expressions of worry could be interpreted not only as individual reactions but also as manifestations of collective apprehension and professional solidarity in times of technological transition, worry, and uncertainty.

Hochschild's (1983) framework also helps to explain why some journalists expressed worry alongside a sense of professional responsibility. Several participants articulated both fear and cautious optimism, signaling a negotiation between internal emotions and external expectations to adapt. As Wharton (2009) argues, such emotional balancing is characteristic of emotional labor, wherein individuals reconcile private concerns with institutional expectations. This dynamic is particularly salient in journalism, where sustaining a forward-looking, adaptable professional disposition is essential to address evolving industry demands (Örnebring, 2018).

1.1 Positive and Regulated Responses

In contrast to expressions of concern, eight participants (five men and 3 women) expressed positive emotions about AI, framing it as a tool with the potential to enhance journalistic practice. However, even within these optimistic responses, a degree of emotional complexity remains. For example, CM1 remarked, "I feel very good about AI. Sometimes I also feel fear, but in a positive way." This response exemplifies what Hochschild (1983) terms *deep acting*, a form of emotional labor in which individuals seek to genuinely align their internal emotional states with the outward emotions they are expected—or wish—to convey. In other words, emotions function as signals for interpreting experiences or situations, and these signals are mediated by individuals' expectations about themselves and the external world. As a result, Hochschild (1983, p.223) argues, "when we do not feel emotion, or disclaim an emotion, we lose touch with how we actually link inner to outer reality."

In addition, fear is acknowledged but reinterpreted as a source of motivation, suggesting that AI's disruptive potential may also be harnessed for professional growth and innovation. This type of emotional reframing aligns with expectations within the journalism field that value adaptability and resilience traits that have been emphasized in prior studies of newsroom cultures and professional identity in times of change (Wasserman, 2018; Forja-Peña et al., 2024).

Despite the ongoing uncertainties surrounding AI, BM2 expressed a sense of calm, attributing this tranquility to an understanding of AI as "part of a historical process of transformation in media." This perspective suggests a form of cognitive reappraisal, in which uncertainty is reframed not as a threat but as a continuation of journalism's longstanding tradition of adaptation and change. Such positive reframing functions as an emotional regulation strategy that helps mitigate fear by positioning AI as an inevitable progression rather than a disruptive force. This approach aligns with Bonanno and Burton's (2013) concept of *regulatory flexibility*, which highlights the importance of adapting emotional regulation strategies to meet situational demands as a means of fostering psychological resilience.

While some journalists expressed genuine enthusiasm—using terms such as "good," "very good," and "positive" to describe their feelings toward AI—others appeared to engage in more adaptive emotional responses. As Wharton (2009) and Bonanno and Burton (2013) suggest, these reactions may reflect regulatory mechanisms in which initial feelings of fear or uncertainty are transformed into curiosity, excitement, or cautious optimism. Through techniques such as *surface acting* and *deep acting* (Hochschild, 1983), journalists may be experiencing internal tensions between the disruptive nature of technological change and the professional imperative to remain adaptable. These emotionally regulated responses could serve not only to maintain composure but also to align with prevailing narratives of innovation and adaptability in journalism's evolving relationship with AI.

Interestingly, two journalists seemed to exhibit ambivalence or uncertainty about their emotional stance toward AI and struggled to identify their feelings; CM2 response about feeling "challenged and good" highlights a tension between apprehension and opportunity where the challenge presented by AI is viewed as a positive force for professional growth, but it is still accompanied by discomfort—being outside of the comfort zone—that is in line with the results obtained by the Thomson Reuters Foundation study (2025). Similarly, MM1 confessed to feeling "uncomfortable, out of sync," suggesting that he is struggling to keep pace with AI's integration in the newsroom. This discomfort reflects the challenges many journalists face as they experience the complexities of a rapidly changing technological environment in consonance with the results obtained by the Financial Times Strategies (2025) where the lack of training and time are often reported as blockers for further adoption.

Another relevant aspect to consider from the emotional responses gathered in this study is that women tend to express more negative feelings and maintain a greater distance toward artificial intelligence (AI), in contrast to men, who demonstrate a more positive attitude and greater openness to engaging with such technologies. In this regard, the findings align with those presented by Armurat et al. (2024, p. 39), who observe that "men perceive AI applications more positively than women, " indicating a significant gender gap in AI perception also in alignment with the findings of Movarec et al. (2024). These results are further corroborated by Russo et al. (2025), whose study shows that women reported higher levels of AI-related anxiety, lower positive attitudes toward AI, lower use of AI, and lower perceived knowledge of AI compared to men.

These findings suggest that gender differences in attitudes toward AI are not only statistically significant but may also have a tangible impact on the adoption and integration of AI technologies in professional settings, including journalism. Recognizing and addressing these disparities is essential for the design of inclusive and equitable AI training programs that can effectively support all practitioners while mitigating biases in implementation and usage.

1.2 "I Like But..."

A recurring answer among the 28 journalists interviewed was the qualified statement "I like AI, but" expressed by 18 participants. This phrase could encapsulate a pattern of cautious acceptance, in which journalists acknowledged the potential benefits of artificial intelligence while simultaneously expressing reservations about its implications. These responses may reflect a dual orientation recognition of AI's utility and concern over its implementation, ethical risks, and potential impact on journalistic integrity and labor conditions.

Analyzed through the lens of Hochschild's (1983) concept of *emotional labor*, the phrase "I like AI, but" illustrates a complex negotiation between internal emotional responses and external professional expectations where the respondents manage their emotions to conform the media organization by performing feelings they may not entirely experience. In the context of AI integration, this negotiation manifests in journalists' attempts to maintain a professional posture of openness and adaptability, even as they harbor doubts, fear, or uncertainties. For instance, statements such as "I like it, but I proceed with caution" (AF1) and "I like it, but I do not fully trust it" (CM1) exemplify this tension between embracing technological innovation and preserving journalistic values. These expressions are indicative of emotional regulation strategies used to reconcile the desire to remain relevant in a changing industry with concerns about ethics, job displacement, and regulatory uncertainty.

Furthermore, qualifying remarks—such as "I like it, but I'm not convinced about how things will unfold" (AM1) and "I like it, but I fear that it will replace professionals" (BF2) suggest the operation of *surface acting* or *deep acting* (Hochschild, 1983). In surface acting, individuals display emotions that are not genuinely felt, while in deep acting, they attempt to align internal emotions with expected expressions. These strategies reveal how journalists are managing affective responses in ways that both reflect and respond to the evolving discourse around AI in journalism.

The call for regulation, as expressed across various interviews, also reflects a *collective emotional response* shaped by shared professional values and uncertainties. As Örnebring (2018) notes, journalists often engage in a process of "making sense of the new normal, " and in this context, emotional labor is performed through efforts to articulate concern without alarmism. This positioning echoes the findings of Forja-Peña et al. (2024) and aligns with Hochschild's (1983) idea of *deep acting*, wherein individuals reconcile personal anxieties with institutional responsibilities, internalizing emotions that are congruent with professional norms.

Moreover, the emphasis placed on ethics and governance illustrates how journalists regulate emotional responses within the framework of professional integrity. The rapid pace of AI adoption—often outstripping the development of regulatory safeguards—has intensified emotional labor, compelling journalists to manage the tension between embracing innovation and safeguarding core journalistic principles. Their calls for more robust regulatory frameworks—in line with the Paris Charter on AI in Journalism (Reporters Without Borders, November 2023), represent attempts to establish both emotional and professional equilibrium, ensuring that the integration of AI aligns with ethical standards rather than undermines them (Porlezza, 2023).

The perspectives shared by FM2 and SM2 further reflect this complex, negotiated stance toward AI. These journalists acknowledged the potential benefits of AI while emphasizing the need for critical reflection and cautious implementation. FM2's statement "I like it, I am not against AI, but I also find it important to maintain a critical perspective on it" highlights the internal balancing act between professional adaptability and ethical skepticism. This response exemplifies *surface acting* as defined by Hochschild (1983), while also resonating with Freire's (1970) concept of *critical consciousness* and Adell's (2006) critique of uncritical technological adoption. Together, these perspectives illustrate how emotional labor, ethical reflection, and pedagogical insight converge in journalists' navigation of AI's evolving role in the profession.

The insistence of both FM2 and SM2 on maintaining a critical stance aligns with Freire's (1970) concept of *critical consciousness*, which emphasizes the necessity of reflective engagement with social and technological change. Their responses indicate that, rather than passively adapting to AI as an inevitable development, they advocate for an informed, participatory approach that interrogates the implications of AI for journalistic ethics, truth-telling, and the integrity of media practices. This perspective also resonates with the findings of Sonni et al. (2024), who highlight concerns about the "black box" nature of algorithmic decision-making in journalism and the importance of transparency as a foundational ethical principle. Moreover, the perspectives offered by FM2 and SM2 support Adell's (2006) caution that uncritical enthusiasm for new technologies can obscure their inherent risks. Their emphasis on critical engagement reflects a broader commitment to responsible AI implementation, one that acknowledges the potential for algorithmic bias, epistemological opacity, and the erosion of journalistic standards. These concerns are echoed in the work of Cardaş-Răduţa (2024) and Nah et al. (2023), who warn that the unchecked integration of AI could undermine key journalistic values. FM2's statement reinforces Adell's position that technological progress must be accompanied by a clearly articulated ethical framework a position further supported by Gutiérrez-Caneda et al. (2024), who argue that media professionals must be central actors in shaping how such frameworks are conceived and applied.

In this context, journalists' responses suggest that while they may publicly endorse artificial intelligence (AI) as an inevitable aspect of journalism's evolution, they continue to wrestle internally with its broader implications. This tension appears to reflect an effort to balance professional adaptability with personal apprehension reinforcing Hochschild's (1983) argument that emotional labor is often necessary in professions where individuals must regulate their feelings to align with organizational or industry expectations.

1.2.1 *Adaptation and Acceptance of Change*

In contrast to those who expressed caution or skepticism, a smaller group of journalists (n = 2) framed their responses in terms of necessary adaptation to an unavoidable technological shift. Statements such as "Whether or not I like it is irrelevant; AI is happening, and we must adapt" (USF2), and "I don't dislike it. As a journalist, I cannot choose whether I like AI or not—it is something that is happening to humanity" (MF2), exemplify a form of *surface acting* where adaptation is performed as a professional obligation rather than as a personally embraced conviction. These expressions reflect an internalized sense of inevitability, whereby resistance is suppressed, and emotional labor is enacted to maintain coherence between professional identity and the perceived technological future of journalism.

This emotional negotiation also aligns with *deep acting* (Hochschild, 1983), in which individuals attempt to reshape their internal emotions to align with external expectations, reducing the discomfort. In doing so, these journalists signal their willingness to adapt, even if their internal perspectives remain unsettled. From a Freirean (1970) perspective, such responses may indicate *an acceptance* of technological change without critical reflection or dialogical engagement. Freire's critique of the "banking model" of education warns against uncritical assimilation of dominant ideologies. In this case, journalists' framing of AI as an unavoidable force reflects accommodation to "*technological determinism*"

(Adell, 2006) where change is treated as externally imposed rather than as something that should be questioned, debated, and shaped through participatory discourse.

1.2.2 I Don't like it

The explicit rejection of artificial intelligence (AI) by journalists such as FM1 and FF1 illustrates a conscious refusal to engage in the emotional labor of forced acceptance and they could be aligned to Kusch (1975, p.111) when he explains that through a dialectical process of negation individuals affirm their existence by engaging with their environment and community: *"Negation has something of a voluntary decision, of sacrifice, of surrender, and for that very reason, of affirmation."* Instead, these journalists express discomfort and professional disillusionment. FM1's statement, "I don't like it; I believe we are losing focus on journalistic production because of all this," reflects a concern that AI integration disrupts core journalistic processes such as investigative rigor, editorial judgment, and creative storytelling. Within Hochschild's (1983) framework, such expressions of negative emotion in professional settings often carry social and institutional risks, as they run counter to dominant narratives that frame AI as a necessary and inevitable advancement. This tension also reflects Adell-Segura's (2010) warning that technological enthusiasm and the need to advance into a digital competence.

Rather than endorsing the uncritical adoption of AI tools, these journalists advocate for a more reflective and ethically grounded framework, one that ensures AI serves journalistic integrity rather than undermining it (Olanipekun, 2025). Their resistance suggests a conflict between long-standing professional identities and perceived pressures to conform to AI-driven newsroom practices. SM1's reflection "I don't like it; I suppose it is connected to my age and my perceptions of what constitutes 'good journalism'" highlights the generational dimension of this emotional negotiation. Hochschild (1983) argues that emotional responses in professional settings are closely tied to self-concept, and in this case for more experienced journalists, AI may symbolize a departure from the principles and practices that define their vocational ethos. This generational context supports O'Brien and Linehan's (2019) argument that emotional labor is not only about managing feelings but also about negotiating shifts in professional identity in response to structural and technological change.

Journalists like SF2, who expressed concerns about the lack of regulation, offer a critique that aligns with both Pierson et al.'s (2023) analysis of European Union policy gaps in AI governance and Freire's (1970) notion of "*critical consciousness.*" From this perspective, resistance to AI is not simply opposition to change but a call for ethical oversight, transparency, and democratic engagement. SF2's position suggests a desire for AI implementation to be embedded within robust regulatory frameworks—an approach echoed by Sánchez-García et al. (2025), who emphasize the importance of participatory policymaking in technological domains.

2 Cross-Cultural Perspectives

Responses from journalists across the seven nations reveal a shared recognition of artificial intelligence (AI) as a transformative force within the media industry. While there is some optimism regarding AI's potential to enhance efficiency and support journalistic work, this enthusiasm is often tempered by caution concerning its limitations and ethical risks. In line with Pavlik (2019), many journalists acknowledge that the continued integration of AI will fundamentally reshape journalistic practices, making the preservation of ethical standards essential for maintaining the societal role and integrity of the profession.

The perspectives gathered reflect a negotiated balance between adaptation and skepticism, shaped by emotional labor (Hochschild, 1983), critical consciousness (Freire, 1970), and reflexive resistance to uncritical technological adoption (Adell, 2006). While journalists see AI as a tool that can streamline repetitive or time-consuming tasks—hereby enabling more in-depth investigative reporting (Deuze & Beckett, 2022)—their responses reveal a broader emotional and professional negotiation. As such, AI is not uniformly perceived as either a competitor or a collaborator (Peña-Fernández et al., 2023), but more often as a *support tool* that must be critically managed (Tejedor et al., 2023)

2.1 AI Rapid Far-Reaching Impact

Across all countries included in this study journalists articulated a growing awareness of AI's rapid and far-reaching impact. Approximately 80% of participants described the integration of AI into journalism as inevitable. However, many participants (AF1; BM1; SF1; USF2) drew historical parallels with earlier technological disruptions—such as the advent of computers, the internet, and social media—as a way of framing AI not as an existential threat but as part of journalism's ongoing evolution. This *historical reframing strategy* serves as an emotional coping mechanism (Bonanno & Burton, 2013), enabling journalists to place AI within a broader continuum of change, thereby maintaining a sense of professional continuity and control. These responses also suggest an understanding of the cyclical nature of technological innovation within media industries (Orihuela, 2019).

In addition to this historical contextualization, the accelerated pace of AI development has triggered deeper reflections on time, adaptability, and the pressures exerted by technological acceleration. Several journalists voiced concerns about the mismatch between the speed of AI evolution and their capacity for informed education, a theme that resonates with Kusch's (1970) distinction between *ser* and *ser-estando*: the former denoting a grounded, stable mode of being, and the latter indicating a presence that is open to waiting, contemplation, silence, and being with others, rather than above others; it is an existential and communal notion in which the human being is not defined by what they produce, but by how they relate to their environment: material, symbolic, and spiritual. The philosopher will define this *ser-estando* as:

> "*Ser* is linked to serving, being worth something, possessing, dominating, and origin. To *be* requires a scaffold of things, undertakings, and concepts—a perfectly organized structure—because without it, no one would be anybody. *Estar*, on the other hand, is linked to situation, place, condition, or mode—that is, to a lack of structure, merely a simple reference to the bare fact of having been born, without knowing why, yet feeling a strange solidity in this alone, a mystery with ancient roots". (Kusch, 1962, p. 426)

The emotional toll of this acceleration is evident in statements such as "I feel like I'm missing the train" (AF2) and "It's all moving too fast" (MF2; SM1), which suggest a perceived lack of space for reflection, learning, and ethical evaluation. This experience of being in a constant state of catch-up illustrates a key contradiction: while AI promises efficiency, it simultaneously imposes a relentless pace of professional transformation that may limit opportunities for meaningful engagement. As Papp (2025) notes, this condition of perpetual adaptation challenges journalistic stability and identity.

Moreover, several journalists voiced concern that the motivation behind AI fast adoption is often driven more by economic imperatives than by journalistic values. As Sjøvaag (2024) argues, the market-driven logic behind AI implementation may prioritize cost-cutting and scalability over editorial quality. This concern is supported by de Lima-Santos and Cerón (2022), who highlight how commercial pressures can distort the ethical mission of journalism, reducing innovation to a tool for profitability rather than for public service. In this context, the fear is not only about how AI is being integrated but why with many journalists calling for critical scrutiny of the institutional motivations that drive AI adoption in newsrooms.

2.2 *Support vs. Supplant*

Journalists' recognition of artificial intelligence (AI) as both a transformative and unpredictable force highlights the emotional labor required to manage its integration into their professional routines. Drawing on Hochschild's (1983) framework, many journalists appear to engage in forms of *surface* or *deep acting* as they cope with their emotional responses to AI within the broader expectations of adaptability in the media industry. Statements such as "This is just the beginning" (CF1) and "It is a tool that is improving day by day, but we cannot fully rely on it" (CM2) could also illustrate a nuanced emotional negotiation expressing cautious optimism while acknowledging the limitations of the technology. This duality may reflects *deep acting*, wherein journalists internally align their emotions with professional norms while maintaining a critical outlook (García-Orosa, 2024).

A recurring sentiment among respondents was the value of their professional instincts, often referred to as a "good nose for news" (De Maeyer, 2020). However, emotional labor is particularly evident in the testimonies of journalists who voiced concerns about job displacement and the broader ethical implications of AI implementation (Upadhyay et al., 2024). Statements such as "AI could replace human workers" (BM1, FF1, AF2) and "Without adequate regulation, AI could lead to reduced job quality and insecurity" (SM2) reveal an emotional tension between fear of obsolescence and professional resilience (Forja-Peña, 2024). In these cases, *surface acting* becomes evident, as some journalists outwardly accept AI as part of the profession's future while internally wrestling with apprehension regarding its implications. This dynamic underscore how emotional labor extends beyond the technical adjustment to AI; it also encompasses the cognitive and emotional processes through which journalists rationalize AI's growing presence within their occupational identity.

A consistent theme across the interviews is the insistence that AI should enhance—rather than replace—human journalistic labor. Statements such as "AI is a tool, and we must be clear that it is not meant to replace our work" (CM2), "AI tools will benefit journalism in some ways, but not in all" (FM1), and "AI can assist but cannot replace the human aspects of reporting" (MM2, AM1, MF2) reflect a resistance to uncritical technological integration. This perspective is consistent with Adell's (2006) and to previous studies (Gutiérrez-Caneda et al., 2024; Sonni et al., 2024). In resisting this trend, journalists advocate for preserving human-centered ethics, editorial autonomy, and the integrity of storytelling amid rapid technological change—an approach that aligns with the principles outlined in the *Paris Charter on AI and Journalism*, produced by Reporters Without Borders (2023), which asserts that human agency must remain central in editorial decisions.

Another significant aspect to highlight is that journalists from Latin America—Argentina, Brazil, and Mexico—have expressed the perception that their counterparts in Western countries may benefit from earlier and more extensive access to AI tools, as well as the prior integration of these technologies into media organizations. This differential access is seen as contributing to more informed perspectives and the establishment of regulatory frameworks in those contexts. However, concerns regarding the adoption of AI in journalism are not confined to countries with limited technological resources or training infrastructure.

For their part, journalist from Europe—France and Spain—have raised critical concerns about the absence of prior consultation regarding their professional needs, the lack of dialogue and preliminary diagnostic assessments, and the ethical ambiguities associated with AI implementation. These issues extend beyond technical limitations and reflect structural and epistemological tensions in the way AI is introduced into journalistic practice. Journalists emphasized their ethical responsibility to audiences, particularly the need to ensure transparency in the use of AI in news production and to maintain editorial integrity. In this regard, the concept of otherness, as articulated by Levinas (1979), provides a valuable ethical framework. Levinas emphasizes the asymmetrical nature of the relationship with the Other, where ethical responsibility is not derived from knowledge or systems but is immediate and unconditional. As he states, "The Other is not a threat, but a responsibility. Responsibility for the Other precedes all theoretical knowledge" (Levinas, 1985, p. 95). This notion aligns with journalists' reflections across both Latin American and European contexts, where AI is understood not merely as a tool to be adopted, but as a development that must be mediated through transparency, ethical discernment, and participatory dialogue as argued by Freire (1970, p.93): "Without dialogue there is no communication, and without communication there can be no true education."

3 Ethics and Training

Ethical concerns voiced by journalists have emerged consistently throughout this study, appearing as a cross-cutting theme across the various topics explored. This sustained presence reveals a deep engagement with the normative responsibilities of the journalistic profession. The interviews suggest that artificial intelligence (AI) is not perceived merely as a technical innovation or an economic strategy, but rather as a profoundly ethical issue that intersects with broader questions of labor, truth, and democratic accountability. As demonstrated throughout this analysis, such ethical reflections align with Levinas's (1985) philosophy, which centers on the primacy of responsibility for the Other. Levinas challenges utilitarian or regulatory conceptions of ethics, arguing instead for a relational and affective understanding of ethical responsibility. Within the journalistic context, this responsibility extends beyond professional duties to encompass obligations toward the audience, society at large, and the integrity of the field itself. Journalists, as mediators of public knowledge, bear a distinctive ethical charge to ensure that the implementation of technological innovation—particularly AI—advances the public good rather than undermines it.

Several journalists explicitly linked ethical concerns to regulatory gaps, noting that insufficient oversight could result in diminished journalistic integrity. This aligns with the findings of Amponsah and Ataniashie (2024), who argue that robust regulatory frameworks are essential to safeguard ethical standards in AI-mediated news production. SM2's observation "Without adequate regulation, AI could lead to reduced job quality and insecurity in the industry," further highlights the need to assess AI's broader impact on labor conditions within journalism. From a Levinasian perspective, this concern reflects an ethical imperative to consider not only the outputs of journalism but also the well-being of those producing it. This concern was echoed by journalists such as AF2, BM1, and FF1, who noted that AI was already replacing human workers, particularly in editorial and content-generation roles. These changes raise critical ethical questions about whether increased efficiency should come at the cost of human livelihoods.

Within the ethical and regulatory framework, four women—two from Spain and two from the United States—voiced specific concerns about the environmental impact of the indiscriminate use of artificial intelligence (AI), with all four participants emphasizing the urgent need to foster greater environmental awareness within the field. This concern reflects what Rodolfo Kusch (1970) refers to as *ser-estando*, a mode of being rooted in presence, contemplation, and coexistence rather than productivity. The perspectives shared by these female journalists reveal how their ethical engagement with AI is shaped not only by technical considerations but also by how they relate to their environment: materially, symbolically, and spiritually. Their expressions of environmental responsibility embody a form of *ser-estando* that foregrounds ethical awareness, care for collective well-being, and a resistance to purely instrumental logics. In addition, as previously discussed, this emphasis articulated by the four journalists illustrates the gender-based differences observed in this study, which may reflect broader patterns in technological use, risk perception, and life quality factors that intersect with gendered experiences in professional settings. These differences underscore the need for further inquiry into how gender shapes journalists' attitudes toward the environmental implications of AI.

The concern and awareness expressed by these women align with the findings of Khajeh Naeeni and Nouhi (2023), who explain that AI presents multifaceted environmental effects, including high energy consumption, increased electronic waste, and the need for sustainable design. Their research emphasizes the necessity of robust policy frameworks and heightened public awareness to mitigate these environmental impacts. Similarly, van Uffelen et al. (2024) explore the ethical dimensions of AI's ecological consequences, advocating for the inclusion of environmental justice in broader discussions of AI ethics. Complementing these views, Chakraborty (2024) proposes a comprehensive framework for monitoring AI's environmental footprint using satellite data and energy metrics, with the objective of informing public policy and promoting sustainability. Taken together, these perspectives suggest that the deployment of AI in media environments must be critically examined not only for its labor implications but also for its ecological consequences especially as automation becomes increasingly integrated into newsroom operations.

Taken together, the emphasis placed by journalists on ethics, regulation, and responsibility suggests that professional development and training initiatives must extend beyond the technical dimensions of AI use. Journalists require critical, transdisciplinary frameworks that equip them to evaluate the broader implications of AI, including its potential to reinforce structural inequities, compromise editorial independence, or erode public trust. Training should therefore incorporate ethical reasoning, social accountability, and reflexive practice, enabling media professionals to engage with AI in a way that sustains journalism's normative commitments. In this context, AI integration must be guided not only by technological innovation or market logic but also by journalism's democratic and public-serving mission.

3.1 *Education on AI: Perspectives by Country*

An analysis of journalists' perspectives across multiple countries reveals several recurring themes related to education and training in artificial intelligence (AI). A key concern expressed by participants was the widespread lack of formal training within media organizations. The absence of structured educational programs was consistently identified as a significant barrier to the effective and ethical integration of AI into journalistic practice. Journalists frequently voiced frustration with the accelerated pace of AI adoption, often describing it as premature given the inadequate institutional support for training and professional development.

While some journalists reported taking individual initiative to learn about AI tools and their implications—through self-guided learning or informal networks (e.g., BF2, USM2) many others emphasized the absence of organizational infrastructure to support such efforts (e.g., AF1, FF2, BM1, MM1). This disparity points to a broader structural issue within newsrooms and media institutions, where the integration of advanced technologies is not being met with a corresponding investment in critical, accessible, and inclusive training.

Regarding Argentina, the concern presented about AI advances and the lack of training is echoed in the work of Lopezosa et al. (2023), who advocate for the development of pedagogical frameworks that prepare journalists to operate ethically and critically in AI-mediated environments. Participants consistently emphasized the need for transdisciplinary training that brings together technology experts and news professionals, ensuring that journalists do not become overly dependent on AI tools but are equipped to assess their risks and benefits (Aliabadi et al., 2023; Salgado, 2022). This collaborative approach supports the development of critical competencies that enable journalists to retain editorial autonomy while adapting to technological change.

Brazilian journalists also reported limited access to formal AI training within media organizations, often turning to external workshops or engaging in self-directed learning. Concerns were raised regarding the inaccessibility of such training, particularly for professionals lacking the financial resources to pursue external courses an issue that echoes the findings of Parrat-Fernández et al. (2024). A recurring theme among participants was the call for comprehensive training that extends beyond technical proficiency to include critical understanding of AI's broader implications, such as algorithmic bias, misinformation, and ethical dilemmas. Three journalists advocated for partnerships with public universities to improve access and quality of training programs. This recommendation aligns with Trattner et al. (2022), who emphasize the importance of interdisciplinary collaboration. Also, perspectives on government involvement in AI regulation were mixed; while some participants supported a state role in guiding ethical frameworks, others expressed concerns about the potential for political influence on AI policy. These concerns resonate with Pierson et al. (2023), who propose a multi-level governance framework to address the complexity of AI policy. In response to these challenges, some journalists favored the idea of "media self-regulation, " as suggested by Sánchez-García et al. (2025), to safeguard editorial independence and ethical integrity.

In China, artificial intelligence (AI) training is offered within media organizations, though it is typically optional rather than mandatory. Despite its voluntary nature, many journalists elect to participate, reflecting a proactive orientation toward professional development. This engagement suggests a recognition of the need to adapt to evolving technological landscapes. Nevertheless, concerns persist regarding overreliance on AI, particularly among younger journalists, whose limited professional experience and uncritical use of AI tools may pose significant challenges to journalistic standards and practices. These concerns are consistent with the findings of Gómez-Diago (2024), who highlights the urgency of integrating core competencies—such as data collection, automated content production, and verification—into journalism education to support the responsible and effective use of AI in newsrooms. One journalist interviewed underscored the dangers of placing blind trust in technological tools, advocating instead for critical engagement and evaluative thinking.

French journalists reported varied experiences with artificial intelligence (AI) training; while some had received instruction, others had not. A recurring concern was the lack of communication between technology departments and editorial teams, which led to perceptions of imposition and discomfort. One journalist described the absence of dialogue regarding the necessity and purpose of certain technological applications as disempowering, reinforcing a top-down dynamic. This disconnect contradicts the principles of critical pedagogy, which emphasize participation and dialogue as argued by Freire (1970, p.80): "Because dialogue is an encounter among women and men who name the world, it must not be a situation where some name on behalf of others. It is an act of creation; it must not serve as a crafty instrument for the domination of one person by another." It also echoes the tensions identified by Gutiérrez-Caneda et al. (2024) between technological advancement and journalistic practice, particularly in terms of preserving professional autonomy. Furthermore, participants expressed a strong need for structured and formalized training aimed at enhancing journalists' ability to identify misinformation and understand AI's potential biases. This aligns with the findings of Nah et al. (2023), who emphasized the importance of proactive engagement by media organizations in developing ethical and educational frameworks around AI.

In Mexico, the limited availability of formal artificial intelligence (AI) training for journalists underscores broader systemic inequalities, particularly those related to disparities in digital infrastructure and access to professional development opportunities (Dunn et al., 2024). Participants expressed concern that Mexico may be falling behind in AI adoption, emphasizing the importance of incorporating ethical dimensions into training efforts, a position consistent with the recommendations of Al-Zoubi et al. (2024). There was also a notable call for a human-centered approach to AI integration. In line with Martínez Navarro's (2025) research, participants voiced concerns about the potential for dehumanization, underscoring the need for critical and conscious engagement with AI in journalistic contexts. This perspective reinforces the importance of designing training frameworks that not only teach technical skills but also encourage ethical reflection and professional responsibility.

Spanish journalists reported a general absence of formal training in artificial intelligence (AI), with several participants suggesting that such training should be optional and tailored to individual professional needs. This perspective aligns with the findings of Fernández-Barrero et al. (2024), who emphasize the importance of flexible, context-sensitive approaches to AI education within the Spanish media landscape. There was also consensus among interviewees on the importance of raising awareness about the limitations and biases embedded in AI technologies (Cardas-Răduţa, 2024). Several participants advocated for training initiatives grounded in diagnostic assessments of journalists' actual needs, incorporating humanistic and social dimensions. This aligns with Freire's (1970) pedagogical framework, particularly his assertion that education must serve as "the practice of freedom the means by which men and women deal critically and creatively with reality and discover how to participate in the transformation of their world" (p. 34). The importance of an ethical approach to AI integration—also observed in other countries analyzed in this study is supported by recent scholarship, including García et al. (2025), Porlezza et al. (2024), and Túñez-López et al. (2024), all of whom highlight the role of normative and institutional safeguards.

In the United States, formal training in artificial intelligence (AI) remains limited among journalists, many of whom rely on informal learning methods such as online tutorials, webinars, and peer recommendations. One journalist emphasized that training should not be framed as a burden or an obligation to adopt new tools, but rather as an opportunity grounded in autonomy and critical engagement. According to this view, training programs should allow for individual choice and prioritize ethical reflection over purely technical skill acquisition. This perspective resonates with Levinas's (1969) ethical philosophy, which emphasizes responsibility and responsiveness toward the Other including technological "others" that mediate journalistic practices. Furthermore, it aligns with Wenger et al. (2024), who argue that fostering ethical sensitivity and critical reflexivity is essential for cultivating media practitioners capable of navigating the epistemological and moral complexities associated with AI and other emerging technologies.

3.2 *Cross-Country Shared Patterns*

While the national contexts of Argentina, Brazil, China, France, Mexico, Spain, and the United States each exhibit specific dynamics regarding AI integration in journalism, a cross-country comparison reveals notable convergences and critical divergences. At the core of this comparative insight is the recognition that journalists across regions are grappling not only with technological adaptation but also with profound ethical, emotional, and structural challenges. These challenges are shaped by unequal access to training, fragmented institutional support, and the tension between innovation and journalistic integrity and ethics as reflected in the study conducted by Amponsah and Ataniashie (2024).

A recurring theme across Argentina, Brazil, and Mexico is the lack of institutionalized AI training, prompting journalists to rely heavily on self-education. This reflects what Freire (1970) describes in "Pedagogy of the oppressed" where professionals are denied the dialogical and emancipatory spaces necessary for critical consciousness. In these countries, journalists voice strong concerns about dependency, misinformation, and dehumanization; concerns that echo Levinas's (1969) ethical imperative to respond to the Other with responsibility and care.

In contrast, countries like China and the United States show greater availability of AI training though often optional and informal. Chinese journalists exhibit a proactive stance toward upskilling but express concern over the uncritical adoption of AI by younger professionals. This highlights Adell's (1997) critique of "false progressivism," where enthusiasm for new technologies risks overshadowing ethical reflection. Similarly, American journalists value autonomy and self-regulation yet express a desire for training grounded in ethical rather than technical paradigms. These perspectives align closely with Levinas's (1969) emphasis on critical engagement with the Other.

France and Spain reveal yet another axis of tension: the fragmentation between technical departments and editorial teams (France), and the defense of autonomy over standardized training (Spain). The absence of interdepartmental dialogue in France signals a breakdown in horizontal communication what Freire (1970) warns against as vertical imposition devoid of true dialogue. Spain's journalists, while similarly undertrained, advocate for humanistic and diagnostic approaches to training, reinforcing both Freire's and Adell's calls for participant-centered education.

Across all seven countries, ethical awareness consistently emerges as a key concern. Journalists repeatedly expressed the need to address AI's opacity, its potential for bias, and the erosion of editorial autonomy. The widely used metaphor in Spanish journalists of AI as a "kitchen knife"—capable of great utility or great harm—captures this duality.

Thus, the shared call across national contexts is for a pedagogical and ethical reframing of AI training in journalism—one that is dialogical (Freire, 1970), ethically responsive (Levinas, 1969), and critically reflexive (Adell, 1997). The future of AI integration in journalism does not rest on technological mastery alone but on the collective ethical dimension, where journalists' expressed feelings of tension—externalized by some and nuanced by others—reveal an unresolved conflict within this field. Adaptation to a situation that exceeds the capacities of communication professionals emerges as a coping mechanism that allows them to "surf" these changes individually. However, this coping strategy also demonstrates that the conflict becomes more burdensome when carried in isolation, without dialogue, as advocated by Freire, or a communal *ser-estando*, as suggested by Kusch (1970).

Therefore, training programs and regulatory frameworks could be more inclusive, transdisciplinary, and critically informed. They should be co-constructed with journalists, rather than imposed from above, enabling media professionals to engage with the tensions between AI-driven efficiency and the human responsibility of storytelling. Nevertheless, crossing borders—intellectually and institutionally—does not in itself resolve this internal conflict; rather, dualities and individual responses continue to dominate, preventing the development of a concrete, community-based dialogue, as will be further explored in the following section.

4 The Value of Imperfection in AI: Ethical, Social, and Technological Dimensions

An analysis of journalists' perspectives across the seven countries reveals several recurring perceptions related to education and training in artificial intelligence (AI). A key concern expressed by participants was the widespread lack of formal training within media organizations. The absence of structured educational programs was consistently identified as a significant barrier to the effective and ethical integration of AI into journalistic practice. Journalists frequently voiced frustration with the accelerated pace of AI adoption, often describing it as premature given the inadequate institutional support for training and professional development.

While some journalists reported taking individual initiative to learn about AI tools and their implications—through self-guided learning or informal networks (e.g., BF2, USM2)—many others emphasized the absence of organizational infrastructure to support such efforts (e.g., AF1, FF2, BM1, MM1). This disparity points to a broader structural issue within newsrooms and media institutions, where the integration of advanced technologies is not being met with a corresponding investment in critical, accessible, and inclusive training.

Similarly, the preference for participatory, critical education is in line with Adell (2006) critical pedagogy, which advocates for training environments that are dialogical, inclusive, and intellectually stimulating. Journalists interviewed in this context stressed the importance of fostering curiosity, critical thinking, and active engagement with the broader implications of AI use in journalism.

Moreover, journalists in six of the countries (Argentina, Brazil, France, Mexico, Spain, and United States) highlighted the necessity of developing accessible and inclusive training opportunities. Many proposed that partnerships between media organizations and educational institutions could serve as effective mechanisms for bridging existing knowledge gaps. Journalists also emphasized the importance of being actively involved in shaping both the content of these training programs and the regulatory frameworks that will govern AI's implementation in the media sector.

These perspectives are reflected in the two primary categories derived from the analysis: the Humanized Diagnostic Media Approach (HDMA) and Critical Transparency and Informed Disclosure (CTID). The HDMA category includes journalists who articulate concerns about the integration of AI, adopting a critical stance while expressing their apprehensions openly and constructively. The CTID category encompasses professionals who foreground the ethical dimensions of AI, emphasizing the need for transparency and ethical literacy among practitioners, journalism students, and the broader audience. It is important to note that these categories are not mutually exclusive; rather, they represent complementary and intersecting dimensions of a broader discourse on the ethical, inclusive, and contextually sensitive integration of AI technologies within journalism.

Throughout the analysis, a tension or internal conflict experienced by more than half of the interviewed journalists becomes evident and recurrent. This psychological and professional discomfort can be meaningfully interpreted through the theoretical lens of Johan Galtung's (1996) conflict mediation framework, particularly his contributions to peacebuilding and the contributions of imperfect peace, which will be discussed in greater detail in the conclusion. For now, the focus will remain on understanding the conflict and its potential mediation.

Galtung (1996) introduces the Conflict Triangle, also known as the ABC Model, which identifies three interrelated components inherent to all conflicts:

- Attitude (A) refers to the perceptions, emotions, and prejudices held by the parties involved. In this study, journalists expressed a wide range of emotional responses—from discomfort and fear to ambivalence and cautious optimism. These affective reactions were often exacerbated by educational shortcomings, employment precarity, and a lack of open dialogue within media organizations, reinforcing negative perceptions of AI integration.
- Behavior (B) encompasses actions taken during the conflict, whether confrontational or cooperative. The journalists' actions included voicing their needs for proper training, ethical guidelines, and expressing a collective critical perspective. These behaviors reflect not only resistance but also attempts to engage constructively with the changes imposed by AI technologies.
- Contradiction (C) represents the underlying structural conditions and root causes of the conflict. In the present context, structural inequalities within media institutions—such as inconsistent access to AI training, absence of ethical frameworks, and top-down implementation of technology—contribute significantly to the tension. These contradictions shape both journalists' attitudes and behaviors, illustrating how a lack of institutional support impacts their sense of agency and well-being.

According to Galtung (2004), this form of conflict resolution goes beyond traditional compromise by addressing the deep-rooted needs of all parties, aiming for transformative, sustainable solutions. Unlike Western "win-lose" paradigms, Galtung's approach promotes "win-win" outcomes that restructure relationships and confront underlying injustices.

Understanding journalists' conflicts regarding AI implementation through this framework offers valuable insights. Galtung (2000) emphasizes that peacebuilding must be rooted in cultural and contextual specificity, incorporating local traditions, narratives, and historical awareness which is in line with Kusch (1970). Applying this model to the journalistic field may facilitate a form of media peacebuilding, where institutional transformations are grounded in ethical inclusion, participatory dialogue, and the recognition of professional and emotional needs.

Regarding peace, Galtung (1969, 1996) introduced the foundational distinction between *positive peace*—defined by the presence of social justice and equity—and *negative peace*, understood as the mere absence of direct violence. Within this conceptual continuum, the notion of *imperfect peace* arises as a transitional or evolving state one that is neither fully immersed in violent conflict nor completely realized in the ideal conditions of positive peace.

Expanding upon these foundational ideas, scholars such as Mac Ginty (2006, 2010) have further developed the framework of imperfect peace, emphasizing its inherent tensions, contradictions, and incompleteness. Drawing from this theoretical lineage, the concept of an *imperfect AI* may be proposed, understood as a condition of partial or ongoing transformation in the media sector. In this state, elements of disruption may persist, even as certain efforts are made to address foundational concerns such as ethical use, access to training, and institutional adaptation.

Building on Galtung's (1996) assertion that peace should not be conceptualized as a binary condition (i.e., war versus peace), but rather as a dynamic and multifaceted process, it can similarly be argued that artificial intelligence (AI) ought not to be understood in reductive terms as either a threat or a solution. Instead, it should be approached as a *processual and dynamic phenomenon*, shaped by the complex and evolving interactions between human actors and algorithmic systems. In this light, the introduction of AI into journalistic environments may either alleviate or intensify tensions depending on the *conditions of its implementation,* particularly the degree to which training, regulation, and dialogical processes are included or omitted in its adoption.

This framework suggests that the implementation of artificial intelligence (AI) in journalism should not be evaluated solely in terms of technological efficiency (Adell, 2006, 2010) or productivity outcomes. Rather, it should be approached through a broader lens of mediated transformation, one that accounts for the ethical, social, and cultural complexities of newsroom integration. This perspective draws on principles of ethical communication (Levinas, 1985), the emotional and professional well-being of media workers (Hochschild, 1983), inclusive and participatory dialogue between journalists and technical teams (Freire, 1970), and culturally situated practices (Kusch, 1970). Collectively, these elements contribute to what may be conceptualized as a peace-oriented approach to technological change, an approach that foregrounds equity, sustainability, and human dignity in the adoption of AI. These critical insights will be further developed in the concluding chapter, which outlines the study's key findings and implications for journalism, education, and future research Fig. 1.

This figure conceptualizes the epistemological tensions that underpin the integration of artificial intelligence (AI) into journalistic practice, framed through the lens of *Imperfect AI*. The horizontal axis represents

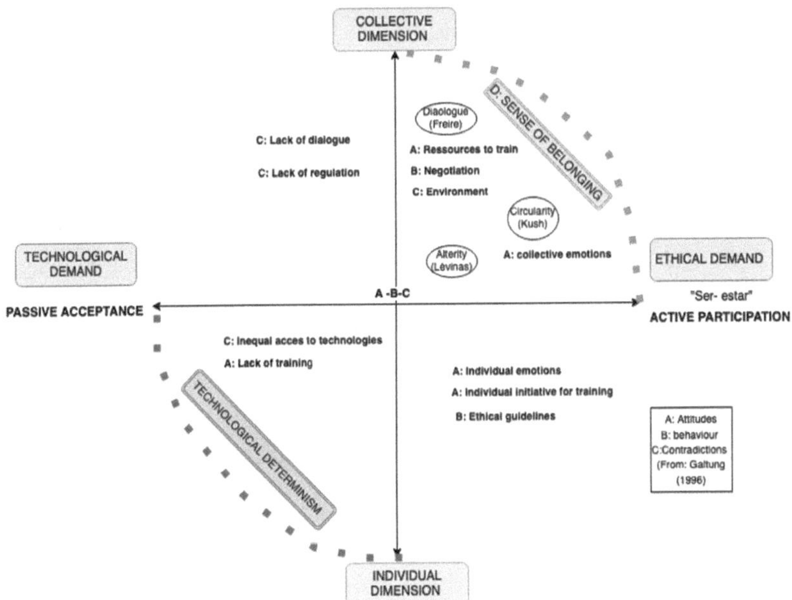

Fig. 1 Epistemological orientation for understanding AI integration in journalism: "Imperfect AI". *Source* Own elaboration. Based on the theoretical contributions of Adell (2006), Freire (1970), Levinas (1969), Kusch (1970, 2012), and Galtung (1996).

the conditions under which AI is implemented in journalistic settings. Drawing on Kusch's (1970) notion of ideology as the "ground"—in this study from which technologies emerge—the axis maps the tension between a technological demand for efficiency and productivity, and an ethical demand for participation and dialogue. These demands manifest in journalists' experiences with AI in their daily work, often revealing contradictions between institutional objectives and professional values and needs.

On the individual level, this tension reflects a conflict between ethical reflection (*ser–estando*) and technical proficiency, the latter often shaped by dynamics of technological determinism (Adell, 2006). On the collective level, the conflict appears as a struggle between a shared ethical call for regulation—articulated through unions and journalists' associations—and the market-driven logic that often dictates AI implementation, such as cost-reduction and scalability (Sjøvaag, 2024). Here, editorial quality is frequently subordinated to commercial imperatives.

The vertical axis captures the tension between individual and collective dimensions, a theme that emerged consistently in this study. These tensions can be analyzed through Galtung's (1996) conflict triangle framework as follows:

1. Emotions: The tension between culturally embedded interpretations of AI and personal emotional responses to its implementation.
2. Ethical Demand: The gap between individual and collective engagement with ethical questions and regulatory responses.
3. Training Demand: A divide between individual efforts to self-train and the broader call for institutional resources to support group-based learning.
4. Emotional Labor: The reconciliation of private apprehensions with organizational expectations, exemplified through surface and deep acting (Hochschild, 1983).
5. Expressions of Worry: The convergence of personal uncertainty and professional solidarity in moments of technological disruption.

The concept of Imperfect AI arises from these overlapping tensions. It positions the journalist at the intersection of individual technological adaptation and collective ethical engagement. Levinas' (1969) ethical imperative—responding to the Other with responsibility—finds concrete expression in journalists' sense of belonging and their accountability to audiences.

From a peace-oriented framework for technological transformation, a more ethical and inclusive approach to AI is possible through a transdisciplinary model of training and reflection. Such a model must be rooted in journalistic experience, and guided by dialogue, emotional awareness, reflective practice, and normative ethical guidelines. Ultimately, this space becomes an opportunity for critical consciousness (Freire, 1970) and the realization of an ethical imperative: to respond with responsibility and care to the audience in the age of artificial intelligence.

CHAPTER 5

Conclusion

Abstract This concluding chapter synthesizes the emotional, ethical, and institutional dimensions explored throughout the study on journalists' responses to the integration of artificial intelligence (AI) into their professional practice. It highlights the complexity and nuance of emotional reactions, from curiosity to skepticism, and examines the tension between adaptability and ethical responsibility in a rapidly evolving technological environment. Through the conceptual frameworks of Humanized Diagnostic Media Approach (HDMA) and Critical Transparency and Informed Disclosure (CTID), the chapter proposes an alternative, reflexive model for understanding AI adoption: *Imperfect AI*. Drawing on peace-oriented mediation theories and relational ethics, it frames AI integration as an ongoing, situated, and culturally contingent process. Rather than viewing technology as a flawless solution, this model emphasizes continuous dialogue, emotional awareness, and ethical accountability. The chapter ultimately advocates for a human-centered, participatory approach to technological change in journalism, where imperfection is not a failure but a generative space for critical reflection, resilience, and responsible innovation.

Keywords Adaptative capacities · Imperfect AI · Emotional awareness · Emotional narratives · Mediating AI · Circularity · Human-centered journalism

© The Author(s), under exclusive license to Springer Nature Switzerland AG 2025

C. Escudero, *Mediating Imperfect AI*,
https://doi.org/10.1007/978-3-032-01290-6_5

As I write this conclusion, the voices and experiences of the interviewed journalists emerge with renewed presence and immediacy. It is possible that, since the time of the interviews, some participants have revised their perceptions or positions regarding artificial intelligence (AI), while others may have reinforced their initial viewpoints. Still others may now be navigating new professional trajectories in the context of ongoing geopolitical transformations.

What becomes clear from this study is that journalists' emotional responses to AI are neither uniform nor static. Rather, they are deeply nuanced and shaped by a constellation of factors including training access, organizational culture, personal values, and ethical considerations. Emotions expressed by the participants span a broad spectrum from worry, concern, and distrust to curiosity, enthusiasm, and cautious optimism. These varied responses underscore not only the adaptive capacities of media professionals, but also the need to consider emotional labor as a critical dimension in understanding how journalists engage with technological transformations.

By foregrounding these emotional narratives, this research contributes to a more comprehensive understanding of AI's impact on journalistic practices. It advocates for institutional frameworks that recognize the value of emotional reflection, support collaborative dialogue between journalists and technology teams, and promote ethical, inclusive, and culturally grounded approaches to training and implementation. As artificial intelligence continues to expand, organizations such as Reporters Without Borders (2023) are actively promoting initiatives like the Paris Charter, which aim to establish clear regulations and grant journalists a central role in responding to these technological developments.

While many journalists express feeling uncomfortable or outdated in response to AI's impact on their roles and the broader media industry, others approach the technology with caution and curiosity, aiming to understand and integrate it responsibly (Objective 1). A smaller subset embraces AI as a catalyst for innovation and transformation, perceiving it as an inevitable element in the ongoing evolution of journalism. Yet, while adaptability is indeed essential in a rapidly changing media landscape, responses that position AI as an unstoppable force—rather than a tool subject to critical scrutiny and regulation—reveal a fundamental tension between professional survival and ethical responsibility. Hochschild's (1983) framework of emotional labor provides a valuable lens to understand how journalists regulate and perform emotions in alignment with institutional expectations, even when those emotions do not fully reflect internal states. In this context, some adaptive mechanisms were not only consciously employed by journalists but were also implicitly expressed in their reactions to AI adoption, aligning with Smith and Lazarus's (1990) cognitive-motivational theory of emotion, which emphasizes the appraisal process in emotional response and coping behavior (O1).

Furthermore, responses to the direct question of whether journalists "like" or "dislike" AI illustrate a spectrum of emotional and cognitive positions ranging from cautious optimism to skepticism and outright rejection. While the majority acknowledged the potential benefits of AI, their answers were often qualified, indicating concerns regarding its implications for journalistic practice, job stability, and the pressing need for regulatory and ethical oversight. In this regard, more than half of the interviewees responded with variations of "I like it, but...," a phrase that captures the unresolved tension underlying their attitudes. This duality reveals a conflict rooted in ethical ambiguity, insufficient regulation, and the inherent biases of AI systems each cited as sources of concern. Thus, the expression "I like..." may be interpreted as a strategic adaptation to a global technological shift, an acknowledgment of a reality that is already shaping professional norms, while the trailing "but" signals the emergence of ethical and practical tensions that remain unaddressed (O1).

This dynamic is aligned with Hochschild's (1983) notion of emotional labor and also resonates with Wharton (2009), in which individuals adjust their expressed attitudes to align with external pressures, even when internal ambivalence persists. In the case of journalists navigating AI integration, the interplay between acceptance and resistance illustrates an emotional negotiation that is shaped by broader institutional forces. These findings underscore the necessity of advancing inclusive, dialogical, and ethically grounded frameworks for AI implementation in journalism.

1 External Pressures

In terms of journalists' perspectives on AI's rapid pace, this reflects a broader struggle between imposed adaptation and meaningful professional engagement and highlights the danger of unquestioning acceptance. In that sense, Adell (1996) warns that the technology acceleration may not necessarily equate to meaningful progress if it is not accompanied by deliberate, reflective integration (O2). The challenge lies in finding ways to engage with AI that preserve journalistic identity and values while resisting the uncritical pressures of speed-driven technological change.

Overall, journalists across cultures emphasize the importance of adopting a balanced perspective regarding the integration of artificial intelligence (AI) in journalism. While AI is recognized for its potential to improve efficiency and support various journalistic tasks, there is also a consistent awareness of its limitations and inherent biases (O2). Most journalists underscore the necessity of comprehensive training, ethical considerations, and regulatory frameworks to ensure the responsible and context-sensitive use of AI technologies in media environments (O3). A dominant theme that emerges is the belief that AI should function as a complementary tool rather than a replacement for journalists. In this view, AI can enhance journalistic workflows by increasing productivity while still safeguarding essential human values such as investigative depth, creativity, and ethical judgment. As the media industry continues to evolve alongside AI, a historically grounded and reflective approach—that critically engages with both the opportunities and the risks of technological innovation—appears to be fundamental for navigating this transformation (O3).

At the same time, the testimonies of journalists from seven countries reveal that the adoption of AI in journalism is not merely a matter of innovation or technological progress; rather, it is a profound ethical responsibility. The concerns articulated by the participants reflect a demand for inclusion, dialogue, and care in the implementation of AI systems, which resonates strongly with Levinas' (1969, p. 75) ethics of the Other: "The face of the Other is the irreducible presence of the Other; it signifies an ethical summons, a demand that cannot be ignored." From this perspective, ethical responsibility begins with the recognition of the Other's presence, calling for an approach to AI that is centered on human dignity, transparency, and participatory regulation. The journalists' emphasis on critical reflection, participatory training, and ethical guardrails suggests a collective yearning for a model of technological adoption that honors human presence in decision-making processes and foregrounds the relational dimension of journalistic labor (O3).

Moreover, the ongoing transformation of journalism, propelled by emerging technologies, serves as a constant reminder of the field's structural and existential tensions. As echoed in many of the testimonies, the evolution of journalism seems to confront professionals with their own limitations, both individually and institutionally. This evolving landscape reminds us that a linear understanding of technological progress may obscure more complex processes of disruption, adaptation, and ethical negotiation. Instead, what may prove more constructive is a broader epistemological orientation—one that encourages professionals to reposition themselves critically, to unlearn entrenched habits, to relearn through collective inquiry, and to reconnect with foundational ethical values and a shared sense of belonging.

In this study, as in previous research, a dichotomy has been observed in journalists' emotional responses to artificial intelligence (AI), often articulated through statements such as "I feel good and positive about AI" or "I feel worried and threatened." This emotional polarization is both significant and indicative of broader professional sentiments. However, the most recurrent expression has been "I like AI, but" revealing an underlying tension and contradiction with which journalists are actively grappling. This ambivalence offers valuable insight into the latent and complex conflict surrounding AI integration in the newsroom its current applications, future potential, and the expectations it generates among media professionals. Although it is necessary to recognize and engage with this tangible, familiar dichotomy as Umberto Eco (1964) notably did in *Apocalyptic and Integrated*, where he examined opposing positions toward mass culture remaining fixed within this binary framework risks oversimplifying the issue. As demonstrated throughout this study, the testimonies collected go beyond this emotional dualism, offering valuable insights and demands that pave the way for actionable solutions. These expressed needs and concerns serve as a starting point for designing responses that address the emotional, professional, community, and ethical dimensions of technological impacts in journalism. This approach not only acknowledges the coexistence of skepticism and enthusiasm but also emphasizes the importance of developing frameworks that facilitate meaningful dialogue, collective adaptation, and critical engagement with AI, thereby fostering a more inclusive and sustainable path forward.

In this context, the notion of *circularity* as articulated by Kusch (1976) through the concept of *ser-estando* offers a profound alternative to linear modern rationality that implies recurrence, reflection, and integration, valuing the return to origin and the dialogical process of knowledge. This view is an invitation to understand human experience not as a forward-driven trajectory, but as a rhythmic, situated, and relational becoming a way of being that is always in relation to place, time, and community.

Moreover, this circular logic resonates with Levinas's (1961) philosophy of otherness, which does not reduce the Other to a category of difference but instead places the ethical relation at the foundation of subjectivity. For Levinas, the Other is not an epistemological object to be classified but an ethical event that interrupts the self and calls it to responsibility. In this way, otherness signifies an infinite ethical demand that resists being absorbed by systems of representation. It invites openness, the willingness to be disrupted, and a response grounded in care—especially in the face of emerging technologies and evolving professional practices.

Within this framework, the categories identified in the present study—Humanized Diagnostic Media Approach (HDMA) and Critical Transparency and Informed Disclosure (CTID)—reflect journalists' efforts to reclaim ethical agency in an AI-mediated media landscape. HDMA highlights the importance of needs-based training and diagnostic assessments that prioritize context, emotional well-being, and ethical sensitivity. CTID, in turn, emphasizes the obligation to disclose the limitations and biases of AI tools, advocating for transparent, critically informed media education. Both perspectives challenge reductionist narratives of technological neutrality, calling instead for participatory, culturally responsive, and ethically grounded forms of integration. These insights support a rethinking of AI not merely as a technological issue but as a relational and epistemological negotiation that aligns with the principles of *imperfect AI* and demands reflexivity, accountability, and care in both professional practice and institutional governance by understanding and embracing conflicts and tensions.

Applying this to the current media environment, the presence of AI—and the emotional labor surrounding its implementation—must not be addressed solely through technical or instrumental lenses. By integrating Kusch's ontological circularity and Levinas's ethical alterity, we may begin to build a more grounded and humane model of media transformation—one that acknowledges the temporal, emotional, and ethical textures of journalistic life and productions. Such an approach not only respects the complexity of AI's integration under a critical perspective (Adell, 1996) into the field, but also re-centers human dignity in working spaces (Hochschild, 1983), relational ethics (Levinas, 1969), through a transformative dialogue (Freire, 1970).

2 Mediating Imperfect AI

The concept of *imperfect AI* can be meaningfully interpreted through Galtung's (1996) ABC model of conflict, which conceptualizes conflict as the interaction between Attitudes (A), Behaviors (B), and Contradictions (C), three interrelated components that contribute to both the escalation and resolution of conflict. In the context of journalism and the integration of artificial intelligence (AI), these elements provide a valuable framework for understanding the tensions, emotional responses, and structural disparities that emerge in response to technological change. Therefore, these categories would be structured as follows:

Attitudes (A) refer to the emotional responses, perceptions, and expectations of journalists regarding AI adoption. As revealed through qualitative interviews, journalists expressed a complex mix of emotions—ranging from anxiety and skepticism to cautious optimism—stemming from both their personal experiences and the structural conditions of their profession. This dimension is particularly illuminated by the work of both Galtung (1996) and Kusch (1979), who argue that emotions and social imaginaries are culturally situated and must be considered when analyzing professional practices. In this case, emotional attitudes are shaped not only by access to resources or training but also by the broader sociopolitical and cultural environment in which journalism operates.

Behaviors (B) encompass the actions that journalists take in response to these emotional and structural tensions. These include voicing demands for inclusive training, advocating for the implementation of ethical guidelines, organizing collective discussions through unions or professional associations, and resisting unilateral top-down impositions of AI tools. Whether these actions are confrontational or cooperative, they reflect active engagement with the technological transformation rather than passive acceptance or rejection. As such, these behaviors suggest a willingness to mediate, negotiate, and transform conditions collectively (Galtung, 2000).

Contradictions (C) refer to the structural conditions and unresolved historical tensions that underlie current challenges. In the context of artificial intelligence (AI), these contradictions manifest in unequal access to technology, the absence of institutional dialogue, and the lack of ethical and pedagogical frameworks for implementation. These issues have frequently been voiced by the journalists consulted, often captured in the expression, "I like AI, but…". This ambivalence reflects not only emotional polarization but also deeper epistemic and institutional concerns. The concept of *ser-estando* (Kusch, 1979)—an ontological position that emphasizes being as a situated, evolving presence—provides a valuable lens through which to interpret this tension. It suggests that journalists are not merely reacting to AI as a fixed technological object but rather engaging with it from a dynamic and historically situated position that reflects their professional identities, cultural contexts, and ethical commitments. All of this also aligns with Galtung's (2002) model of peace journalism, which encourages journalists to serve as agents of conflict transformation by emphasizing empathy, contextual understanding, and a focus on solutions.

To further enrich this model within the field of journalism studies, and based on the results of this study, I propose the addition of a fourth dimension: Sense of Belonging (D). This extension acknowledges the increasing body of evidence suggesting that a journalist's emotional resilience and professional engagement are deeply influenced by their perceived inclusion within a team or institutional culture (Escudero, 2024c; Maares et al., 2023). The *D* dimension foregrounds the affective ties that shape journalists' capacity to navigate transformation, cope with emotional stress, and contribute meaningfully to ethical media practices.

By incorporating this fourth element, the adapted ABCD model allows for a more comprehensive and human-centered understanding of *imperfect AI* in journalism that considers not only structural conditions and behaviors but also the emotional and relational dimensions necessary for fostering sustainable, collective responses to technological disruption. In this case, the sense of belonging emerges as a critical affective and organizational factor. As Maares et al. (2023) have shown, journalists who experience a strong sense of belonging within their teams are often better equipped to confront professional and emotional challenges. This sense of collective identity can foster dialogue and shared ethical consciousness (Freire, 1970), whereas its absence may reinforce fragmentation, isolation, and emotional exhaustion. Addressing the vulnerability of belonging in journalistic environments becomes, therefore, not only a matter of well-being but also a necessary step toward enabling collective mediation in the face of technological disruption.

Therefore, when emphasizing the concept of *imperfect AI*, this work adopts an epistemological stance that reframes imperfection not as deficiency, but as a condition of being unfinished and in constant formation.

This conceptualization invites a repositioning that fosters more critical and nuanced engagement with the evolving nature of artificial intelligence. In contrast to ideals of perfection, completion, and linear objectives—aspirations that often obscure the complexity of human experience—*imperfect AI* reminds us that our existence is fundamentally shaped by ongoing, unresolved processes, characterized by uncertainty and intricacy, which may give rise to discomfort, tension, and conflict.

Within this framework, *imperfect AI* evokes a state of *being-in-becoming*, or *ser-estando*, a concept rooted in the philosophy of Rodolfo Kusch (1976), which highlights the embodied, relational, and temporally situated dimensions of human existence. This ontological perspective invites a re-humanization of our relationship not only with ourselves and our communities, but also with the spaces, uses, dependencies on technologies we develop and adopt. As such, it opens the possibility for creating *encuentros dialógicos* (dialogical encounters) that serve as spaces of mediation in contexts marked by tension, uncertainty, and ethical ambiguity.

Rather than conceptualizing AI as a totalizing or deterministic force, the notion of imperfection introduces a generative space for reflection, critical questioning, and context-sensitive action. When viewed through this lens, technological integration is no longer reduced to technical or economic imperatives but is reimagined as an ethical and situated process one that must remain attuned to the values, vulnerabilities, and lived realities of the communities it intends to serve. In this polarized landscape, opposing claims—such as "AI is a great opportunity" or "AI will destroy employment"—often become absolute positions, each presented as unquestionable truth. Yet both perspectives reveal a shared condition: the absence of critical doubt. Within the framework of *imperfect AI*, this absence is particularly significant, as it underscores the necessity of embracing ambiguity, fostering reflexivity, and transcending binary thinking. Rather than seeking definitive answers, *imperfect AI* encourages a more nuanced, ethically grounded engagement with technology, one that values uncertainty as a space for dialogue, responsibility, and human-centered inquiry.

The recent growth of and transdisciplinary research on AI in journalism has fostered a proliferation of knowledge exchanges. Increasingly, scholars and practitioners alike emphasize the urgency of transdisciplinary education in AI, an education that considers the intersection of emotional, ethical, technical, and cultural dimensions of media practice. Approaching

AI implementation through the lens of *active mediation* that involves a more engaged, directive roles (Bercovitch and Houston, 2000) in the context of an *imperfect AI* allows us to understand how these transformations may be met with training programs and dialogues that prioritize journalists' needs, perspectives, and humanity.

This pursuit is neither linear nor absolute, but rather circular, dialogical, and continuously evolving through sustained engagement. Rooted in responsibility, critical thinking, and care, the concept of *imperfect AI* envisions a future in which artificial intelligence is not defined by flawless automation, but by ethically grounded integration. It is a future shaped by human values, a space where contradictions and vulnerabilities are recognized and openly discussed, where conflict is not denied but engaged with thoughtfully. These aspirations propose a technological landscape in which AI complements, rather than replaces, the fundamental social mission of journalism: to inform, to question, and to connect in ways that remain profoundly human.

Annexes

Annex 1: In-Depth Interviews—Questionnaire

This interview is part of a scientific research project on the role of artificial intelligence (AI) in journalism. Your participation is entirely voluntary, and all information provided will remain strictly confidential. The data will be used solely for academic and scientific purposes.

Informed Consent

Do you consent to the researcher using your responses within the framework of the study described above?

☐ Yes ☐ No.

Personal Information

(*This information will be used only for follow-up purposes and will not appear in the published study.*)

- **Full Name**:
- **Age**:
- **Gender**:
- **Country and City**:
- **Media Organization**:

© The Editor(s) (if applicable) and The Author(s), under exclusive license to Springer Nature Switzerland AG 2025
C. Escudero, *Mediating Imperfect AI*,
https://doi.org/10.1007/978-3-032-01290-6

Section 1: Professional Background

1. **How many years have you worked as a journalist?**
   (Please indicate the number of years.)

Section 2: Emotions and Experiences with AI in Journalism

1. **How do you feel about the presence of artificial intelligence (AI) in journalism and within your newsroom?**
   (*Please describe your emotional and professional response.*)
2. **Do you like AI?**
   (*Please elaborate on your answer. Feel free to include both positive and negative aspects.*)

Section 3: Organizational Practices and Training Perspectives

3. **Have you received any training related to artificial intelligence?**
   ☐ Yes ☐ No
   - *If yes*: How would you describe the training? Would you be interested in further training?
   - *If no*: Would you be interested in receiving AI-related training in the future?
4. **Do you currently use AI tools or systems in your journalistic work?**
   - *If yes*, please describe how.
   - *What is your general perception of AI in journalistic practice?*
5. **Do you believe media organizations should hold more internal discussions about AI's implications?** (*Please explain your view.*)
6. **In your opinion, how should education and training around AI in journalism be designed?**(*You may select one of the following approaches or suggest your own.*)
   - ☐ **Option A**: A dialogue-based approach that fosters collaboration between media and the scientific/technological community. This model promotes adaptable regulations and aims to empower journalists to engage critically with AI, without feeling overwhelmed.

- ☐ **Option B**: A market-driven model where training responds to evolving industry demands. Journalists are expected to continuously adapt and upskill to remain competitive in a tech-driven landscape.
- ☐ **Other**: (Please specify)

Section 4: Final Reflections

7. Would you like to share any additional comments, insights, or reflections regarding your experience with AI in journalism? (*Feel free to address specific tools, ethical concerns, editorial practices, or personal stories*).

References

Adell, J. (2006). Tendencias en educación en la sociedad de las tecnologías de la información. [Trends in Education in the Information Technology Society]. *Edutec, Revista Electrónica De Tecnología Educativa*, (7), a007. https://doi.org/10.21556/edutec.1997.7.570

Adell, J. (2011, May 1). *Web 2.0 y educación: ¿El «Día de la marmota»?* [Blog post] [Web 2.0 and Education: Groundhog Day Again?].El bonia. https://elbonia.cent.uji.es/jordi/2011/05/01/web-2-0-y-educacion-%C2%BFel-dia-de-la-marmota%E2%80%9D/

Adell-Segura, J. (2010). *La competencia digital en el siglo XXI: Un nuevo marco para la educación.* [Digital Competence in the 21st Century: A New Framework for Education]. In J. P. A. F. de la Torre (Ed.), *La educación en la Sociedad del Conocimiento* (pp. 229–244). Ediciones Sintesis.

Adjin-Tettey, T. D., Muringa, T., Danso, S., & Zondi, S. (2024). The role of artificial intelligence in contemporary Journalism Practice in Two African Countries. *Journalism and Media, 5*(3), 846–860. https://doi.org/10.3390/journalmedia5030054

Ahmad, N., Haque, S., & Ibahrine, M. (2023). The news ecosystem in the age of AI: Evidence from the UAE. *Journal of Broadcasting & Electronic Media, 67*(3), 323–352. https://doi.org/10.1080/08838151.2023.2173197

Ahmed, S. (2004). *The Cultural Politics of Emotion*. Routledge.

Akeran, P. N., Myom, A. B., & Terhemba, S. N. (2024). *Artificial intelligence in journalism: Transforming news production and practice.* Lambert Academic Publishing.

© The Editor(s) (if applicable) and The Author(s), under exclusive license to Springer Nature Switzerland AG 2025

C. Escudero, *Mediating Imperfect AI*,
https://doi.org/10.1007/978-3-032-01290-6

AlAshry, M. S., & Al-Saqaf, W. (2024). Constraints on AI: Arab Journalists' experiences and perceptions of governmental restrictions on ChatGPT. Journal of Information Technology & Politics, 1–21. https://doi.org/10.1080/19331681.2024.2421388

Albizu-Rivas, I., Parratt-Fernández, S., & Mera-Fernández, M. (2024). Artificial intelligence in slow journalism: Journalists' uses, perceptions, and attitudes. *Journalism and Media, 5*(4), 1836–1850. https://doi.org/10.3390/journalmedia5040111

Aliabadi, R., Singh, A., Wilson, E. (2023). Transdisciplinary AI education: The confluence of curricular and community needs in the instruction of artificial intelligence. In (T. Schlippe, E.C.K. Cheng, T. Wang, Eds) Artificial Intelligence in Education Technologies: New Development and Innovative Practices. AIET 2023. Lecture Notes on Data Engineering and Communications Technologies, vol 190. Springer, Singapore. https://doi.org/10.1007/978-981-99-7947-9_11

Al-Zoubi, O., Ahmad, N., & Abdul Hamid, N. (2024). Artificial intelligence in newsrooms: Ethical challenges facing journalists. *Studies in Media and Communication, 12*(1), 401. https://doi.org/10.11114/smc.v12i1.6587

Amponsah, P., & Atianashie, A. (2024). Navigating the new Frontier: A comprehensive review of AI in journalism. *Advances in Journalism and Communication, 12*, 1–17. https://doi.org/10.4236/ajc.2024.121001

Andrade, S., & Molinari, G. (2021, August 3) Las 10 experiencias que pasaron por el taller de autogestión de tiempo. Tiempo Argentino. [The 10 Experiences That Participated in the Time Self-Management Workshop. Tiempo Argentino]. https://www.tiempoar.com.ar/formacion-tiempo/las-10-experiencias-que-pasaron-por-el-taller-de-autogestion-de-tiempo

Archibald, M. M., Ambagtsheer, R. C., Casey, M. G., & Lawless, M. (2019). Using Zoom Videoconferencing for Qualitative Data Collection: Perceptions and Experiences of Researchers and Participants. International Journal of Qualitative Methods, 18. https://doi.org/10.1177/1609406919874596

Armutat, S., Wattenberg, M., & Mauritz, N. (2024). Artificial Intelligence—Gender-Specific differences in perception, understanding, and training interest. In *Proceedings of the 7th International Conference on Gender Research* (Vol. 7, pp. 36–43). Academic Conferences International Ltd. https://doi.org/10.34190/icgr.7.1.2163

Attard, M., Davis, M., and Main, L. (2023) Gen AI and Journalism. Centre for Media

Transition, University of Technology Sydney, Australia. https://doi.org/10.6084/m9.figshare.24751881

Ayyad et al., 2023 Ayyad, K., Ben Moussa, M., & Zaid, B. (2023). Journalists' Perception of the Adoption of New Communication Technologies in the

UAE's Media Organizations. Journalism Practice, 1–21. https://doi.org/10.1080/17512786.2023.23002777

Backholm, K., & Björkqvist, K. (2010). The effects of exposure to crisis on well-being of journalists: A study of crisis-related factors predicting psychological health in a sample of Finnish journalists. *Media, War and Conflict, 3*(2), 138–151. https://doi.org/10.1177/1750635210368309

Barnes, L. (2016). *Journalism and everyday trauma: A grounded theory of the impact from death-knocks and court reporting*. Auckland University of Technology.

Bercovitch, J., & Houston, A. (2000). Why do they do it like this? An analysis of the factors influencing mediation behavior in international conflicts. *Journal of Conflict Resolution, 44*(2), 170–202. https://doi.org/10.1177/0022002700044002003

Bonanno, G. A., & Burton, C. L. (2013). Regulatory flexibility: An individual differences perspective on coping and emotion regulation. *Perspectives on Psychological Science, 8*(6), 591–612. https://doi.org/10.1177/1745691613504116

Borelli, J. (2019). *Rebooting journalism: How media startups overcame the business model crisis. What can we learn from Eldiario.es and Mediapart?* Reuters Institute for the Study of Journalism, University of Oxford. Accessed 19 December 2024 https://reutersinstitute.politics.ox.ac.uk/sites/default/files/2020-02/Rebooting_journalism_Javier_Borelli_Jan_2020.pdf

Bornstein, R. F. (1989). Exposure and affect: Overview and meta-analysis of research, 1968–1987. *Psychological Bulletin, 106*(2), 265–289. https://doi.org/10.1037/0033-2909.106.2.265

Braun, V., & Clarke, V. (2006). Using thematic analysis in psychology. *Qualitative Research in Psychology, 3*(2), 77–101. https://doi.org/10.1191/1478088706qp063oa

Bryman, A. (2016). *Social research methods*. Oxford University Press.

Buchanan, M., & Keats, P. (2011). Coping with traumatic stress in journalism: A critical ethnographic study. *International Journal of Psychology, 46*(2), 127–135. https://doi.org/10.1080/00207594.2010.532799

Cabra, M. (2022, December). The inevitable mental health revolution. *NiemanLab*. https://www.niemanlab.org/2022/12/the-inevitable-mental-health-revolution

Cardaş-Răduţa, D.L. The effectiveness and limitations of artificial intelligence in journalism. (2024) *SAECULUM*, Lucian Blaga University of Sibiu, vol. 57 no. 1, pp. 111–119. https://doi.org/10.2478/saec-2024-0009

Chakraborty, S. (2024). Towards a comprehensive assessment of AI's environmental impact. *arXiv preprint*arXiv:2405.14004. https://doi.org/10.48550/arXiv.2405.14004

Charmaz, K.(2014). *Constructing grounded theory*. Thousand Oaks: SAGE Publications Ltd.

Creswell, J. W. (2014). *Research design: Qualitative, quantitative, and mixed methods approaches*. Sage Publications.

Dandurand, G., McKelvey, F., & Roberge, J. (2023). Freezing out: Legacy media's shaping of AI as a cold controversy. *Big Data & Society*, 10(2). https://doi.org/10.1177/20539517231219242

Dart Center (2008) Resources for PTSD & Trauma. https://dartcenter.org/resources?topic%5B0%5D=70

de-Lima-Santos, M.-F., & Cerón, W. (2022). Artificial intelligence in news Media: Current perceptions and future outlook. *Journalism and Media, 3*(1), 13–26. https://doi.org/10.3390/journalmedia3010002

de Lima-Santos, M., & Salaverría-Aliaga, R. (2021) "From data journalism to artificial intelligence: Challenges faced by La Nación in implementing computer vision in news reporting". Palabra Clave. 24 (3), 2021, e2437. https://doi.org/10.5294/pacla.2021.24.3.7

De Maeyer, J. (2020). A nose for news: From (News) values to valuation. *Sociologica, 14*, 109–132. https://doi.org/10.6092/ISSN.1971-8853/11176

Denscombe, M. (2010). *The good research guide: For Small-Scale research projects*. Buckingham Open University Press.

Denzin, N. K., & Lincoln, Y. S. (Eds.). (2018). *The SAGE handbook of qualitative research* (5th ed.). SAGE Publications.

Deuze, M. (2023). Considering mental health and well-being in media work. *Journal of Media Practice, 24*(2), 123–138. https://doi.org/10.1080/14682753.2023.1934567

Deuze, M., & Beckett, C. (2022). Imagination, algorithms and news: Developing AI literacy for journalism. *Digital Journalism, 10*(10), 1913–1918.

Dewey, J. (1910). *How we think*. D.C. Heath & Co.

Díaz-Lucena, A., & Vicente-Fernández, P. (2023). AI and the human need for emotional connection. In *Revolutionizing communication* (1st ed., Chap. 9). CBC Press, Taylor & Francis Group. https://doi.org/10.1201/9781003473633-9U

Dweck, C. S. (2006). *Mindset: The new psychology of success*. Random House.

Dunn, H. S., Ragnedda, M., Ruiu, M. L., & Robinson, L. (Eds.). (2024). *The Palgrave handbook of everyday digital life*. Palgrave Macmillan. https://doi.org/10.1007/978-3-031-43982-7

Eco, U. (1964). *Apocalípticos e integrados en la cultura de masas*. Lumen.

Elo, S., & Kyngäs, H. (2008). The qualitative content analysis process. *Journal of Advanced Nursing, 62*(1), 107–115. https://doi.org/10.1111/j.1365-2648.2007.04569.x

Eppich, W.J., Gormley, G.J., Teunissen, P.W. (2019). In-Depth Interviews. In: Nestel, D., Hui, J., Kunkler, K., Scerbo, M., Calhoun, A. (Eds) Healthcare Simulation Research. Springer, Cham. https://doi.org/10.1007/978-3-030-26837-4_12

Escudero, C. (2023). Recovered media in Argentina: A resilient response to instability and precariousness. In S. Bebawi & O. Onilov (Eds.), *Different global journalisms* (pp. 63–83). Palgrave Macmillan.

Escudero, C. (2024)a. *El abordaje de la salud emocional en los estudios de Periodismo y Comunicación.* [Addressing Emotional Health in Journalism and Communication Studies]. In *Buenas prácticas universitarias para la mejora del compromiso educativo y social.* [University Best Practices for Enhancing Educational and Social Engagement] *Editorial* Dykinson.

Escudero, C. (2024)b. *La IA en los estudios de periodismo y comunicación: Desafíos y compromisos éticos.* [AI in Journalism and Communication Studies: Ethical Challenges and Commitments]. In Coord. Sara González-Yubero, Buenas prácticas universitarias para la mejora del compromiso educativo y social [University Best Practices for Improving Educational and Social Engagement]. 994–1010. Editorial Dykinson. ISBN 978–84–1070–060–4.

Escudero, C. (2024)c. Transforming crises into opportunities: Self-managed media in Argentina. *Media and Communication, 12*(2), 131–142. https://doi.org/10.17645/mac.7455

Escudero, C., Prola, T. A., Fraga, L., & Flores, E. S. (2023a). Emotional management in journalism and communication studies. *Social Space Journal, 23*(2), 507–524.

Escudero, C., Prola, T., Soriano Flores, E., Silva Alvarado, E. (2023) The Scope of Technostress and Care of The Self on Journalists During the Pandemic. Social Space Journal Volume 23 Issue 042023 https://socialspacejournal.eu/menu-script/index.php/ssj/article/view/285

Escudero, C., & Zhang, E. (2025). How do journalists feel about AI? Insights from seven countries. World of Media. *Journal of Russian Media and Journalism Studies*, 2, pp. 5–32. https://doi.org/10.30547/worldofmedia.2.2025.1.

European Council (2024) Guidelines on the responsible implementation of artificial intelligence systems in journalism; consulted at https://rm.coe.int/cdmsi-2023-014-guidelines-on-the-responsible-implementation-of-artific/1680adb4c6

Feinstein, A., Pavisian, B., Storm, H. (2018) Journalists covering the refugee and migration crisis are affected by moral injury not PTSD. JRSM Open. 2018;9(3). https://doi.org/10.1177/2054270418759010

Fernández-Barrero, M.- Ángeles, López-Redondo, I., & Aramburú-Moncada, L. G. (2024). Possibilities and challenges of artificial intelligence in the teaching and learning process of Journalism Writing. The experience in

Spanish universities. *Communication & Society*, *37*(4), 241–256. https://doi.org/10.15581/003.37.4.241-256

Festinger, L. (1957). *A theory of cognitive dissonance*. Stanford University Press.

Festinger, L., & Carlsmith, J. M. (1959). Cognitive consequences of forced compliance. *Journal of Abnormal and Social Psychology, 58*(2), 203–210. https://doi.org/10.1037/h0041593

Financial Times Strategies. (2025). *Behind the headlines: How journalists really feel about AI*. Retrieved February 22 2025, from https://www.ftstrategies.com/en-gb/insights/behind-the-headlines-how-journalists-really-feel-about-ai

Flannery, R. B. (2022). News journalists and posttraumatic stress disorder: A review of literature, 2011–2020. *Psychiatric Quarterly, 93*, 151–159. https://doi.org/10.1007/s11126-021-09920-z

Flores-Morales, R., Reyes-Pérez, V., Reidl-Martínez, L.M. (2012) Postryaumatic stress symptoms in Mexican journalists covering the drug war. *Suma Psicologica,* [online], *19*(1), 7–17. ISSN 0121-4381.

Forja-Pena, T., García-Orosa, B., & López-García, X. (2024). A shift amid the transition: Towards smarter, more resilient digital journalism in the age of AI and disinformation. *Social Sciences, 13*(8), 403. https://doi.org/10.3390/socsci13080403

Frankl, V. E. (1984). *Man's search for meaning* (I. Lasch, Trans.). Beacon Press. (Original work published 1946).

Frazão Nogueira, A. G. C., & Pinto, R. J. (2024). The resilience of journalistic values. In M. Vaz Álvarez, J. M. Túñez López & A. G. C. Frazão Nogueira (Eds.), *The public value blueprint* (pp. 1–15). Springer. https://doi.org/10.1007/978-3-031-60824-7_1

Freire, P. (1970). *Pedagogy of the oppressed* (M. B. Ramos, Trans.).

Freire, P. (1974). *Education for critical consciousness*. Continuum.

Freire, P. (1976). *Education, the practice of freedom*. Writers and Readers Publishing Cooperative.

Freire, P. (1985). *The politics of education: Culture, power, and liberation* (D. Macedo, Trans.). Bergin & Garvey.

Freire, P. (1996). *Pedagogy of hope: Reliving pedagogy of the oppressed* (R. R. Barr, Trans.). Continuum.

Freire, P. (1998). *Pedagogy of freedom: Ethics, democracy, and civic courage* (P. Clarke, Trans.). Rowman & Littlefield.

Freitas, R. A. & Benetti, M. (2015). Alterity, otherness and journalism: A phenomenological perspective. *PhilArchive*. https://doi.org/10.25200/BJR.v13n2.2017.989

Fredrickson, B. L. (2001). The role of positive emotions in positive psychology: The broaden-and-build theory of positive emotions. *American Psychologist, 56*(3), 218–226. https://doi.org/10.1037/0003-066X.56.3.218

Fromm, E. (2009a). *Buddhism and the mode of having vs. Being* (Original work written 1975). *Fromm forum (English version), (13)*, 31–34. Tuebingen: Selbstverlag. (Published posthumously from the literary estate of Erich Fromm).

Given, L. M. (2016). *100 Questions (and answers) about qualitative research*. Sage.

Galtung, J. (1969). Violence, peace, and peace research. *Journal of Peace Research, 6*(3), 167–191. https://doi.org/10.1177/002234336900600301

Galtung, J. (1996). *Peace by peaceful means: Peace and conflict, development and civilization*. SAGE Publications.

Galtung, J. (2000). *Conflict transformation by peaceful means: The transcend method*. United Nations. https://digitallibrary.un.org/record/255733?v=pdf

Galtung, J. (2004). *Transcend and transform: An introduction to conflict work*. Pluto Press.

García-Avilés, J. A. (2019). El impacto de la inteligencia artificial en el periodismo. Máster en innovación en periodismo [blog] [The impact of artificial intelligence on journalism. Master's in journalism innovation]. Universidad Miguel Hernández. https://l1nq.com/SYGw7

García-Orosa, B., Forja-Pena, T., & López-García, X. (2024). Digital newsroom transformation: A systematic review of the impact of artificial intelligence on journalistic practices, news narratives, and ethical challenges. *Media and Communication, 5*(4), 97–110. https://doi.org/10.17645/mac.v5i4.5514

Gascón, S., Fueyo-Díaz, R., Borao, L., Leiter, M. P., Fanlo-Zarazaga, Á., Oliván-Blázquez, B., & Aguilar-Latorre, A. (2021). Value conflict, lack of rewards, and sense of community as psychosocial risk factors of burnout in communication professionals (press, radio, and television). *International Journal of Environmental Research and Public Health, 18*(2), 365. https://doi.org/10.3390/ijerph18020365

Given, L. M. (2016). *100 questions (and answers) about qualitative research*. Sage.

Grieves, K. (2012). *Journalism across boundaries*. Palgrave Macmillan.

Grimonport, A. (2024, December 6) Exploring RSF's new AI charter for journalism", Reuters Institute, consulted 12 December 2024 at https://reutersinstitute.politics.ox.ac.uk/calendar/exploring-rsfs-new-ai-charter-journalism

Gobo, G. (2008). *Doing ethnography*. SAGE Publications.

Goleatz, K., Bear, F., Katzenbach, C. (2018). *The turn to artificial intelligence in governing communication online*. HIIG Workshop Report. The Alexander von Humboldt Institute for Internet and Society (HIIG). https://bit.ly/3HNdgkH

Guion, L. A., Diehl, D. C., & McDonald, D. (2011). Conducting an in-depth interview: FCS6012/FY393, rev. 8/2011. *EDIS, 2011*(8). https://doi.org/10.32473/edis-fy393-2011

Gutiérrez-Caneda, B., Lindén, C.-G., & Vázquez-Herrerom, J. (2024a). Ethics and journalistic challenges in the age of artificial intelligence: Talking with professionals and experts. *Frontiers in Communication, 9*, 1–10. https://doi.org/10.3389/fcomm.2024.1465178

Gutiérrez-Caneda, B., Vázquez-Herrero, J., & López-García, X. (2023). AI application in journalism: ChatGPT and the uses and risks of an emergent technology. *Profesional De La Información, 32*(5), Article e320514. https://doi.org/10.3145/epi.2023.sep.14

Gutiérrez-Caneda, B., Lindén, C.-G., & Vázquez-Herrero, J. (2024). Ethics and journalistic challenges in the age of artificial intelligence: Talking with professionals and experts. *Frontiers in Communication, 9*, Article 1465178. https://doi.org/10.3389/fcomm.2024.1465178

Harmon-Jones, E., & Mills, J. (Eds.). (2019). *Cognitive dissonance: Reexamining a pivotal theory in psychology*. American Psychological Association.

Harré, R. (1986). *The social construction of emotions*. Blackwell.

Hochschild, A. R. (1983). *The managed heart: Commercialization of human feeling*. University of California Press.

Holas, S. (2017). Rodolfo Kusch's 'Estar' as seen from the systemic perspective of Humberto Maturana as a way of 'corazonar' coexistence. *The Australian Journal of Indigenous Education, 47*(1), 64–72. https://doi.org/10.1017/jie.2017.27

Hughes, S., Iesue, L., Peña, S., & Garcés, M. (2021). Coping with occupational stress in journalism: Professional identities and advocacy as resources. *Journalism*. https://doi.org/10.1177/14648849211018613

Hwang, K.-K. (1987). Face and favor: The Chinese power game. *American Journal of Sociology, 92*(4), 944–974. https://doi.org/10.1086/228588

Hudson, H. (Director). (1981). *Chariots of fire* [Film]. Enigma Productions; Twentieth Century Fox.

Izard, C. E. (1977). *Human emotions*. Springer.

Kaiser, K. (2009). Protecting respondent confidentiality in qualitative research. *Qualitative Health Research, 19*(11), 1632–1641. https://doi.org/10.1177/1049732309350879

Kalfeli, P., & Angeli, C. (2025). The intersection of ai, ethics, and journalism: Greek journalists' and academics' perspectives. *Societies, 15*(2), 22. https://doi.org/10.3390/soc15020022

Khajeh Naeeni, S., & Nouhi, N. (2023). The environmental impacts of AI and digital technologies. *AI and Tech in Behavioral and Social Sciences,1*(4), 11–18. https://doi.org/10.61838/kman.aitech.1.4.3

Kusch, R. (1970). *América profunda*. Editorial Biblos.

Kusch, R. (1975). *La negación del pensamiento popular*. Hachette.

Kusch, R. (1976). *América profunda*. Editorial Bonum.

Kusch, R. (2012). *El pensamiento indígena y popular en América*. Editorial Fundación Ross.

Lang, D. J., Wiek, A., Bergmann, M., Stauffacher, M., Martens, P., Moll, P., & Thomas, C. J. (2012). Transdisciplinary research in sustainability science: Practice, principles, and challenges. *Sustainability Science, 7*(S1), 25–43. https://doi.org/10.1007/s11625-011-0149-x

Lazarus, R. S. (1991). *Emotion and adaptation*. Oxford University Press.

Lema, J. L. (2006). Psicología cultural y las emociones en el contexto latinoamericano. *Revista De Psicología Social, 8*(3), 120–134.

Lermann-Henestrosa, A., & Kimmerle, J. (2024). The effects of assumed AI vs. Human authorship on the perception of a GPT-generated text. *Journalism and Media, 5*(3), 1085–1097. https://doi.org/10.3390/journalmedia5030069

Levinas, E. (1969). *Totality and infinity: An essay on exteriority* (A. Lingis, Trans.). Duquesne University Press.

Levinas, E. (1985). *Ethics and infinity: Conversations with Philippe Nemo* (R. Cohen, Trans.). Duquesne University Press.

Levinas, E. (1998). *Entre nous: On thinking-of-the-other* (M. B. Smith & B. Harshav, Trans.). Columbia University Press.

Löffelholz, M., & Weaver, D (Eds.), (2008) *Global Journalism Research: Theories, Methods, Findings, Future*. Blackwell-Wiley.

López-García, X., & Vizoso, A. (2021). Periodismo de alta tecnología: Signo de los tiempos digitales del tercer milenio. *El Profesional De La Información., 30*(3), 1. https://doi.org/10.3145/epi.2021.may.01

Lopezosa, C., Codina, L., Pont-Sorribes, C., & Vállez, M. (2023). Use of generative artificial intelligence in the training of journalists: Challenges, uses and training proposal. *Profesional De La información, 32*(4). https://doi.org/10.3145/epi.2023.jul.08

Lünenborg, M., & Medeiros, D. (2020). Journalism as an affective institution: Emotional labor and the discourse on fraud at *Der Spiegel. Media and Communication, 8*(3), 5–15. https://doi.org/10.17645/mac.v8i3.3085

Maares, P., Banjac, S., & Nölleke, D. (2023). Newsrooms as sites of community and identity: Exploring the importance of material place for journalistic work. *Journalism Studies, 24*(13), 1611–1628. https://doi.org/10.1080/1461670X.2023.2241074

Mac Ginty, R. (2006). *No war, no peace: The rejuvenation of stalled peace processes and peace accords*. Palgrave Macmillan.

Mac Ginty, R. (2010). Hybrid peace: The interaction between top-down and bottom-up peace. *Security Dialogue, 41*(4), 391–412. https://doi.org/10.1177/0967010610374312

Makwambeni, B., Matsilele, T. and Bulani, J.G. (2023), "*Between Utopia and Dystopia: Investigating journalistic perceptions of AI deployment in community media newsrooms in South Africa*", Dralega, C.A. (Ed.) Digitization, AI and Algorithms in African Journalism and Media Contexts, Emerald Publishing Limited, Leeds, pp. 17–32. https://doi.org/10.1108/978-1-80455-135-620231002

Manfredi-Sánchez, J.L. & Ufarte- Ruiz, M. J. (2020) "Inteligencia artificial y periodismo: Una herramienta contra la desinformación". [Artificial intelligence and journalism: a tool against disinformation] *Revista CIDOB d'Afers Internacionals*, No. 124 p. 49–72. doi.org/https://doi.org/10.24241/rcai.2020.124.1.49

Marconi, F. (2020). *Newsmakers: Artificial intelligence and the future of journalism*. Columbia University Press.

Martínez-Navarro, G. (2025). Artificial intelligence and journalism: Exploring journalists' perspectives. *Doxa Comunicación, 40*, 259–278. https://doi.org/10.31921/doxacom.n40a2717

Martínez, J., & Alvarado, R. (2021). The social construction of emotions in Latin America: Between history, politics, and resistance. *Latin American Perspectives, 48*(2), 32–47.

Méndez-Hernández, L.E., Eufrosino-González, E.G., González, K. (2024) Communication perspective in sports journalism based on Artificial Intelligence, in *Health Leadership and Quality of Life*. 3:.533, pp_1–8. https://doi.org/10.56294/hl2024.533

Mesquita, B., & Frijda, N. H. (1992). Cultural variations in emotions: A review. *Psychological Bulletin, 112*(2), 179–204.

Møller, L. A., Skovsgaard, M., & de Vreese, C. (2024a). Reinforce, readjust, reclaim: How artificial intelligence impacts journalism's professional claim. Journalism, 0(0). https://doi.org/10.1177/14648849241269300

Møller, L. A., van Dalen, A., & Skovsgaard, M. (2024b). A Little of that human touch: How regular journalists redefine their expertise in the face of artificial intelligence. *Journalism Studies, 26*(1), 84–100. https://doi.org/10.1080/1461670X.2024.2412212

Moravec, V., Hynek, N., Skare, M., Gavurova, B., & Kubak, M. (2024). Human or machine? The perception of artificial intelligence in journalism, its socio-economic conditions, and technological developments toward the digital future. *Technological Forecasting and Social Change, 188*, Article 122306. https://doi.org/10.1016/j.techfore.2023.123162

Morse, J.M., Barrett, M., Mayan, M., Olson, K., Spiers, J. (2002). Verification strategies for establishing reliability and validity in qualitative research. *Int. J. Qual. Methods*. 2002;1(2):1–19. https://doi.org/10.1177/160940690200100202.

Munoriyarwa, A. (2024). Unravelling socio-Technological barriers to AI integration: A qualitative study of southern african newsrooms. *Emerging Media, 2*(3), 474–498. https://doi.org/10.1177/27523543241288814

Nah, S., Luo, J., Kim, S., Chen, M., Mitson, R., & Joo, J. (2023). Rethinking artificial intelligence: Algorithmic bias and ethical issues|algorithmic bias or algorithmic reconstruction? a comparative analysis between ai news and human News. *International Journal Of Communication, 18*, 30. Retrieved from https://ijoc.org/index.php/ijoc/article/view/20815

Newman, N. (2021, January 28). Periodismo, medios y tecnología: tendencias y predicciones para 2021. [Journalism, Media, and Technology: Trends and Predictions for 2021] Reuters Institute for the Study of Journalism. University of Oxford https://bit.ly/3HI0t39

Newman, N. (2022). Journalism, media, and technology trends and predictions 2022. The Reuters Institute for the Study of Journalism. https://ti-nyurl.com/5e95d9tu

Newman, N. (2024). Journalism, media, and technology trends and predictions 2024; Reuters Institute, January 9. Available online: https://reutersinstitute.politics.ox.ac.uk/journalism-media-and-technology-trends-and-predictions-2024 (accessed on January 18 2025).

Noain-Sánchez, A. (2022). "Addressing the Impact of artificial intelligence on journalism: The perception of experts, journalists and academics". Communication & Society. 35 (3), pp. 105 – 121. https://doi.org/10.15581/003.35.3.105-121

Noor, R., & Zafar, H. (2023) Use of Artificial intelligence in pakistani journalism: Navigating challenges and future paths in TV newsrooms. *Journal of Asian Development Studies*, 12(3), 1638–1649. https://doi.org/10.62345/jads.2023.12.3.131

Nowell, L. S., Norris, J. M., White, D. E., & Moules, N. J. (2017). Thematic analysis: Striving to meet the trustworthiness criteria. International Journal of Qualitative Methods, 16(1). https://doi.org/10.1177/1609406917733847

Nussbaum, M. C. (2001). *Upheavals of thought: The intelligence of emotions*. Cambridge University Press.

O'Brien, E., & Linehan, C. (2019). Emotions online: exploring knowledge workers' emotional labour in a digital context in an agile IT company. *Human Arenas*. https://doi.org/10.1007/s42087-023-00364-4

Ogola, G. (2025). Between fear and hope: Generative AI, ChatGPT and Journalism. In: Mutsvairo, B., Orgeret, K.S. (Eds) The Palgrave Handbook of Global Digital Journalism. Palgrave Macmillan, Cham. https://doi.org/10.1007/978 3 031 59379 6_13

Olanipekun, S. O. (2025). Ethical frameworks for AI in journalism: Balancing technological innovation and journalistic integrity. *World Journal of Advanced Research and Reviews, 25*(1), 1342–1351. https://doi.org/10.30574/wjarr.2025.25.1.0187

Omona, J. (2013). Sampling in qualitative research: Improving the quality of research outcomes in higher education. *Makerere Journal of Higher Education, 4*, 169–185.

Oxman, C. (1998): La entrevista de investigación en ciencias sociales. [The research interview in social sciences], Buenos Aire: Fundación Xeito Novo. Disponible en

Orihuela, J. L. (2019). The digital transformation of journalism. *Medium*. Retrieved from https://jlori.medium.com/the-digital-transformation-of-journalism-1748c38df2bc

Örnebring, H. (2018). Journalists thinking about precarity: Making sense of the "new normal." *Journalism Studies, 19*(7), 977–991. https://doi.org/10.1080/1461670X.2016.1249007

Pantoja-Lima, S.; Mick, J., Nicoletti, J., Barros, J., Henriques, R., Moliani, J., Patrício, E., Pereira, F & Zacarioti, M. (2022) Perfil do Jornalista Brasileiro 2021. [Profile of the Brazilian Journalist 2021] Florianópolis: *Quorum Comunicações*, 2021. Retrieved November 15 2024: https://perfildojornalista.paginas.ufsc.br/files/2022/06/RelatorioPesqui

Papp J. T. (2025). Adapting to change: AI's potential impacts on journalism. *Pázmány Law Review, 11*(1), 17–31. https://doi.org/10.55019/plr.2024.1.17-31

Parratt Fernández, S., Rodríguez-Pallares, M., & Pérez-Serrano M. J. (2024). Artificial intelligence in journalism: An automated news provider. *Index comunicación*, 14(1), 183 205. https://doi.org/10.62008/ixc/14/01Artifi

Partha, S., Tbassum, M., Goni, A. (2024) Artificial intelligence (AI) and future newsrooms: A study on journalists of Bangladesh, in *Pacific Journalism Review*, Vol. 30, No. 1–2, July 2024, pp. 96–110. ISSN (electronic):2324–2035

Patton, M. Q. (2015). *Qualitative research & evaluation methods* (4th ed.). SAGE Publications.

Pearson, M. & Seglins, D. (2022). Taking Care: A report on mental health, well-being and trauma among Canadian media workers. Canadian Journalism Forum on Violence and Trauma. Retrieved Janurary 21 2025 https://static1.squarespace.com/static/60a28b563f87204622eb0cd6/t/6285561b128d0447d7c373b2/1652905501967/TakingCare_EN.pdf

Pearson, M., McMahon, C., O'Donovan, A., & O'Shannessy, D. (2021). Building journalists' resilience through mindfulness strategies. *Journalism, 22*(7), 1735–1751. https://doi.org/10.1177/1464884919833253

Pekrun, R. (2006). The control-value theory of achievement emotions: Assumptions, corollaries, and implications for educational research and practice. *Educational Psychology Review, 18*(4), 315–341. https://doi.org/10.1007/s10648-006-9029-9

Pereira, F. H., & Mastrella, B. (2022). The practice of data-driven journalism in brazil: Between disruption and the reinstatement of professional Values. *Digital Journalism, 10*(4), 599–625. https://doi.org/10.1080/21670811.2022.2061550

Piasecki, S., Morosoli, S., Helberger, N., & Naudts, L. (2024). AI-generated journalism: Do the transparency provisions in the AI act give news readers what they hope for? *Internet Policy Review, 13*(4). https://doi.org/10.14763/2024.4.1810

Pierson, J., Kerr, A., Robinson, S.C., Fanni, R., Steinkogler, V.E., Milan, S., & Zampedri, G. (2023). Governing artificial intelligence in the media and communications sector. *Internet Policy Review, 12*(1). https://doi.org/10.14763/2023.1.1683

Porlezza, C. (2023). The datafication of digital journalism: A history of everlasting challenges between ethical issues and regulation. *Journalism, 25*(5), 1167–1185. https://doi.org/10.1177/14648849231190232

Porlezza, C., & Schapals, A. K. (2024). AI ethics in journalism (Studies): An evolving field between research and practice. *Emerging Media, 2*(3), 356–370. https://doi.org/10.1177/27523543241288818

Posetti, J., Shabbir, N., Maynard, D., Bontcheva, K. & Aboulez, N. (2021) The chilling: Global Trends in online violence against women journalists. UNESCO. Retrieved, December 20 2024 https://unesdoc.unesco.org/ark:/48223/pf0000377223

Reese, S. D. (2008). *Theorizing a globalized journalism.* En Löffelholz, M. Y Weaver, D. (Eds.), Global Journalism Research: Methods, Findings, Future (pp.240–252). Blackwell.

Repko, A. F., & Szostak, R. (2020). *Interdisciplinary research: Process and theory* (3rd ed.). SAGE Publications.

Reporters Without Borders, (Novemebr, 2023) *Paris Charter on AI and journalism* . Retrieved 21 November 2024 https://rsf.org/en/paris-charter-ai-and-journalism

Rinehart, A., & Kung, E. (2022). Artificial intelligence in Local News: A survey of US newsrooms 'AI readiness (p. 56). The Associated Press.

Rubin, H. J., & Rubin, I. S. (2012). *Qualitative interviewing: The art of hearing data* (3rd ed.). SAGE Publications.

Russo, S., Romano, A., Clemente, F., Iacovone, D., Gladwin, T. E., & Panno, A. (2025). Gender differences in AI adoption: The role of AI anxiety and positive attitudes toward AI. *Frontiers in Psychology, 16*, 1559457. https://doi.org/10.3389/fpsyg.2025.1559457

Salazar, I. (2018). Los robots y la Inteligencia Artificial. Nuevos retos del periodismo. [Robots and Artificial Intelligence: New Challenges for Journalism] *Doxa Comunicación*, 27, pp. 295–315. https://doi.org/10.31921/doxacom.n27a15

Saldaña, J., & Omasta, M. (2018). *Qualitative research: Analyzing life*. SAGE Publications.

Salgado, L. (2022) *From the Classroom to the Newsroom: A critical route to introduce AI in journalism education. Facts and Frictions, 2*(1). https://doi.org/10.22215/ff/v2.i1.04

Salvat-Martinrey, G., García-Marín, D., & Zorogastua Camacho, J. (2024). La inteligencia artificial generativa y su impacto en el sector de la comunicación. Percepción de los futuros profesionales. [Generative Artificial Intelligence and Its Impact on the Communication Sector: Perceptions of Future Professionals] *Revista De La Asociación Española De Investigación De La Comunicación, 11* (Especial), raeic11e06. https://doi.org/10.24137/raeic.11.e.6

Samuel, J., Kasyap, R., Yana, S., & Pelaez, A. (2022). Adaptative cognitive fit: Artificial intelligence augmented management of information facets and representations. *International Journal of Information Management, 65*, Article 102505. https://doi.org/10.1016/j.ijinfomgt.2022.102505

Sánchez-González, H. (2022) Transformación digital y audiencia. Tendencias y uso de la inteligencia artificial en medios verificadores. [Digital Transformation and Audience: Trends and Use of Artificial Intelligence in Fact-Checking Media] *Ámbitos. Revista Internacional de Comunicación | NO. 56 9 – 20*.https://doi.org/10.12795/Ambitos.2022.i56.01

Sánchez-García, P., Diez-Gracia, A., Mayorga, I. R., & Jerónimo, P. (2025). Media Self-Regulation in the Use of AI: Limitation of multimodal generative content and ethical commitments to transparency and verification. *Journalism and Media, 6*(1), 29. https://doi.org/10.3390/journalmedia6010029

Sánchez-Laws, A. L. (2017). Can immersive journalism enhance empathy? *Digital Journalism, 8*(2), 213–228. https://doi.org/10.1080/21670811.2017.1389286

Segura, M. S. (2015). Los medios comunitarios, populares y alternativos de Argentina desde la ley audiovisual: de la lucha por la legalidad al debate sobre la sostenibilidad. [Community, Popular, and Alternative Media in Argentina Since the Audiovisual Law: From the Struggle for Legality to the Debate on Sustainability] *Diálogos de la Comunicación*, 92(12), 1–16.

Segura, M. S., & Waisbord, S. (2016). *Media movements: Civil society and media policy reforms in Latin America*. Zed Books

Serrano-Oceja, J. (2023). From journalists' precarity and mental health to the effects of AI. *Journal of Media and Mental Health, 18*(1), 45–59. https://doi.org/10.1234/jmmh.2023.012

Schiffrin, A. (2024) "AI and the future of journalism: An issue brief for stakeholders", UNESCO consulted at https://unesdoc.unesco.org/ark:/48223/pf0000391214

Shoai, A. (2024). Journalistic training on artificial intelligence in Latin America: Challenges from a collaborative program perspective. *Journal of Media Studies, 23*(2), 157–171. https://doi.org/10.1234/jms.2024.035

Silvia, P. J., & Kashdan, T. B. (2009). Interesting things and curious people: Exploration and engagement as transient states and enduring strengths. *Social and Personality Psychology Compass, 3*(5), 785–797. https://doi.org/10.1111/j.1751-9004.2009.00210.x

Silverman, D. (2017). *Doing qualitative research* (5th ed.). SAGE Publications.

Simon, F. (2023) *La IA no revolucionará el periodismo, pero está lejos de ser una moda pasajera". [AI Will Not Revolutionize Journalism, but It Is Far from a Passing Fad]* Reuters Institute, Oxford University. Retrieved December 19 2024 https://l1nq.com/Y6xjv

Simon, F. (2024). *Artificial intelligence in the news: How AI retools, rationalizes, and reshapes journalism and the public arena.* Tow Center for Digital Journalism, Columbia University. Simon_2024_Artificial_intelligence_in.pdf

Simunjak, M. (2023). Managing emotions in journalism: A guide to enhancing resilience. Cham, Switzerland Palgrave Macmillan.

Sirén-Heikel, S., Kjellman, M., & Lindén, C.-G. (2023). At the crossroads of logics: Automating newswork with artificial intelligence—(Re)defining journalistic logics from the perspective of technologists. *Journal of the Association for Information Science and Technology, 74*(3), 354–366. https://doi.org/10.1002/asi.24656

Sivira-Camacaro, R. (2025). La formación universitaria de periodistas en el contexto de la Inteligencia Artificial: una revisión sistematizada. [University Education of Journalists in the Context of Artificial Intelligence: A Systematized Review] *Doxa Comunicación. Revista Interdisciplinar De Estudios De Comunicación Y Ciencias Sociales, 40*, 513–529. https://doi.org/10.31921/doxacom.n40a2225

Sjøvaag, H. (2024). The business of news in the AI economy. *AI Magazine, 45*(2), 246–255. https://doi.org/10.1002/aaai.12172

Smith, C. A., & Lazarus, R. S. (1990). *Emotion and adaptation*, Chapter 23. In L. A. Pervin (Ed.), *Handbook of personality: Theory and research* (pp. 609–637). Guilford Press.

Smith, J. A., & Doe, R. L. (2024). Impact of AI integration on journalists' mental health: A quantitative analysis. *Journal of Media Psychology, 12*(3), 45–59. https://doi.org/10.1234/jmp.v12i3.5678

Sonni, A. F., Hafied, H., Irwanto, I., & Latuheru, R. (2024). Digital newsroom transformation: a systematic review of the impact of artificial intelligence on journalistic practices, news narratives, and ethical challenges. *Journalism and Media, 5*(4), 1554–1570. https://doi.org/10.3390/journalmedia5040097

Spyridou, P., & Ioannou, M. (2025). Exploring AI amid the hype: A critical reflection around the applications and implications of AI in journalism. *Societies, 15*(2), 23. https://doi.org/10.3390/soc15020023

Stake, R. E. (2005). Qualitative case studies. In N. K. Denzin & Y. S. Lincoln (Eds.), *The SAGE handbook of qualitative research* (3rd ed., pp. 443–466). SAGE Publications.

Storm, H. (2023). Mental health and wellbeing for journalists: A practical guide. *Routledge*. https://doi.org/10.4324/9781003344179

Strauss, A., & Corbin, J. (1990). *Basics of qualitative research* (Vol. 15). Sage Publishing.

Stupart, R. (2021). Feeling responsible: Emotion and practical ethics in conflict journalism. *Media, War & Conflict, 14*(3), 268–281. https://doi.org/10.1177/17506352211013461

Tejedor Calvo, S. (dir.), Pulido, C., Hita, E. y Robledo, K. (2023). La inteligencia artificial en el periodismo. Mapping de conceptos, casos y recomendaciones. [Artificial Intelligence in Journalism: Mapping of Concepts, Cases, and Recommendations] *Revista De Comunicación, 23*(2), 387–388. https://doi.org/10.26441/RC23.2-2024-R2-3507

Thomas, D. R. (2006). A general inductive approach for analyzing qualitative evaluation data. *American Journal of Evaluation, 27*(2), 237–246. https://doi.org/10.1177/1098214005283748(Originalworkpublished2006)

Thomson Reuters Foundation. (2025, January 28). *Journalists cautiously optimistic about AI, our new report finds.* Retrieved February 26 2025, from https://www.trust.org/2025/01/28/journalists-cautiously-optimistic-about-the-effect-of-ai-on-the-profession-our-new-report-finds/

Trattner, C., Jannach, D., Motta, E. *et al.* Responsible media technology and AI: Challenges and research directions. (2022) *AI Ethics* 2, 585–594 (2022). https://doi.org/10.1007/s43681-021-00126-4

TurboScribe. (n.d.). *TurboScribe.ai* [AI transcription service]. Accessed January 26 2025 https://www.turboscribe.ai/

Tyng, C. M., Amin, H. U., Saad, M. N. M., & Malik, A. S. (2017). The influences of emotion on learning and memory. *Frontiers in Psychology, 8*, 1454. https://doi.org/10.3389/fpsyg.2017.01454

Upadhyay A., Bijale, M., Hasan K. (2024) Impact of AI integration on journalists' Mental Health: A Quantitative Study. *Annals of Neurosciences.* 2024;0(0). https://doi.org/10.1177/09727531241278909

Urquhart, C. (2013). *Grounded Theory for Qualitative Research: A Practical Guide.* Sage.

Van Uffelen, N., Lauwaert, L., Coeckelbergh, M., & Kudina, O. (2024). Towards an environmental ethics of artificial intelligence. *arXiv preprint*arXiv: 2501.10390. https://doi.org/10.48550/arXiv.2501.10390

Wahl-Jorgensen, K. (2019). *Emotions, media and politics.* Polity Press.

Wenger, D., Hossain, M. S., & Senseman, J. R. (2024). AI and the impact on journalism education. *Journalism & Mass Communication Educator, 80*(1), 97–114. https://doi.org/10.1177/10776958241296497

Vygotsky, L. S. (1978). *Mind in society: The development of higher psychological processes.* Harvard University Press.

Waisbord, S. (2013). Reinventing professionalism: Journalism and news in global perspective. John Wiley & Sons.

Wasserman, H. (2018). Relevance, resistance, resilience: Journalism's challenges in a global world. *Journalism, 20*(1), 229–232. https://doi.org/10.1177/1464884918809290(Originalworkpublished2019)

Wenger, D., Hossain, M. S., & Senseman, J. R. (2024). AI and the impact on Journalism education. *Journalism & Mass Communication Educator, 80*(1), 97–114. https://doi.org/10.1177/10776958241296497(Originalworkpublished2025)

Wharton, A. S. (2009). The sociology of emotional labor. *Annual Review of Sociology, 35*(1), 147–165. https://doi.org/10.1146/annurev-soc-070308-115944

Wiles, R., Crow, G., Heath, S., & Charles, V. (2008). The management of confidentiality and anonymity in social research. *International Journal of Social Research Methodology, 11*(5), 417–428. https://doi.org/10.1080/13645570701622231

Yu et al., 2020 Yu, Y., Huang, K, and Jones, B. (2020). "Artificial Intelligence in Media: Journalists' Perceptions and Organizational Talk", Communication, technologies et développement. https:// doi.org/https://doi.org/10.4000/ctd.3262

Yu, Y., & Huang, K. (2021). Friend or foe? Human journalists' perspectives on artificial intelligence in Chinese media outlets. *Chinese Journal of Communication, 14*(4), 409–429. https://doi.org/10.1080/17544750.2021.1915832

Zajonc, R. B. (1968). Attitudinal effects of mere exposure. *Journal of Personality and Social Psychology, 9*(2), 1–27. https://doi.org/10.1037/h0025848

Zhou, Y. (2008). Voluntary adopters versus forced adopters: Integrating the diffusion of innovation theory and the technology acceptance model to study intra-organizational adoption. *New Media & Society, 10*(3), 475–496. https://doi.org/10.1177/1461444807085382

FSC
www.fsc.org
MIX
Papier | Fördert gute Waldnutzung
FSC® C083411

Kolibri 360 GmbH
Ferdinand-Jühlke-Straße 7
99095 Erfurt, Deutschland
produktsicherheit@kolibri360.de